Penguin Modern Poets
VOLUME 4

Liz Lochhead was born in Motherwell in Lanarkshire in 1947. She was educated at the Glasgow School of Art, where she trained in the department of Drawing and Painting. Her first book of poems was published in 1972 and since then she has been in great demand on the poetry-reading circuit all over Britain and abroad. Further volumes of poetry have been written, including *Dreaming Frankenstein and Collected Poems*, *True Confessions* and *Bagpipe Muzak*, which is published by Penguin, as are the plays *Mary Queen of Scots Got Her Head Chopped Off* and *Dracula*. She earns her living as a dramatist, broadcaster and performing poet. Apart from extended spells in New York City and Toronto, she has lived for most of her adult life in Glasgow.

Roger McGough, born in Liverpool, has been writing for adults and children for many years, and his numerous collections have established him as one of the most distinctive and powerful voices in contemporary poetry. *The Mersey Sound* (Henri, McGough, Patten), published in 1967, is the only one of the original Penguin Modern Poets series still in print. A further selection, *New Volume*, appeared in 1987. Both volumes of his selected poems (1967–87), *Blazing Fruit* and *You at the Back*, are published by Penguin, as well as his latest collections, *Melting into the Foreground* (1986) and *Defying Gravity* (1992). Apart from two previously unpublished poems, it is from the later books that this selection has been made.

Sharon Olds was born in San Francisco in 1942. Many of her books have been published in the USA, including *Satan Says* (1980), *The Dead and the Living* (1984) and *The Gold Cell* (1987). In Great Britain she has published *The Matter of This World* (1987), *The Sign of Saturn* (1991) and *The Father* (1993). She teaches at New York University, and helps to run the University's writing workshop at the Sigismund Goldwater Memorial Hospital, a public hospital for the severely physically disabled. She lives in New York City.

The Penguin Modern Poets Series

Penguin Modern Poets

VOLUME 4

LIZ LOCHHEAD

ROGER McGOUGH

SHARON OLDS

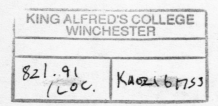
PENGUIN BOOKS

Published by the Penguin Group
Penguin Books Ltd, 27 Wrights Lane, London w8 5tz, England
Penguin Putnam Inc., 375 Hudson Street, New York, New York 10014, USA
Penguin Books Australia Ltd, Ringwood, Victoria, Australia
Penguin Books Canada Ltd, 10 Alcorn Avenue, Toronto, Ontario, Canada m4v 3b2
Penguin Books (NZ) Ltd, Private Bag 102902, NSMC, Auckland, New Zealand

Penguin Books Ltd, Registered Offices: Harmondsworth, Middlesex, England

This selection first published 1995
10 9 8 7 6 5 4 3

Typeset by Datix International Limited, Bungay, Suffolk
Printed in England by Clays Ltd, St Ives plc
Set in 10.5/13pt Monophoto Garamond

Contents

Liz Lochhead

Smirnoff for Karloff

For Marilyn Bowering and Bessie Smith

So you're who's been sleeping in
my bed. Well, hello there.
Long time no see.
So you're my Big Fat Little Secret
stretched out cold,
just between you and me.

Between you and me and the bedpost
it's getting a little crowded in here.
Roll over, let me whisper sweet zeros
in your Good Ear.
Open up your Glad Eye.
Oh my! I'm going to make you.
Going to make you sit up.
Going to make you.
Going to take you to bits.
Going to take you to the cleaners.
Going to make you look cute.
Going to let you roly-pole all over me
in your funeral suit –
The one you wear to weddings. Yeah.
With the too short drainpipe trousers
with the brothelcreeper boots with the
tyre-track soles
and the squirt-in-the-eye trick carnation
in your button-hole.

You know Matron,
take more than hospital corners to keep
a good man down, oh
yeah. Everything
in applepie order.

All present
and correct. Shipshape. Aye-aye.
He got all my wits around him
his extrasensory senses and his
five straight limbs.
Yes sir,
you'll be up and about again
in no time.

What wouldn't you
give to love me? An arm, and a leg?
Going to make you,
make you sit up,
sit up and beg. Hey, Mister,
Mister can your dog do tricks?
Going to make you,
going to put you to the test,
make you give your all six
nights per week and on Sundays
going to take the rest.

Sure, you can smoke in bed.
It's a free country.
Let me pour you a stiff drink.
You're shivering.
Well, you know what they say if you
can't take the cold then get outa
the icebox. What's that?
Smirnoff?
Well, you know, Mr Karloff,
I used to think an aphrodisiac was some
kinda confused Tibetan mountain goat
with a freak-out hair-do until I
met my monster and my monster
met his maker.
Oh yeah.

That who been sleeping in my bed.
Same old surprise. Oh goody.
Long time no see.
Ain't going to let nothing come between
my monster and me.

The Bride

I am the absolute spit of Elsa Lanchester.
A ringer for her, honestly,
down to the zigzag of lightning in my frightwig
and it's funny no one, me in-
cluded, ever noticed the resemblance before
because
this fine morning
jolted awake by a crash in the kitchen
the smell of burning
and the corncrake domesticity of dawnchorus toast
getting scraped, suddenly
there's the me in the mirror staring back at me
and me less than amazed at me all marcelled
like Elsa Lanchester.
Well, it's apt enough,
this is my last morning as a
single girl.

Despite your ex-wife's incendiary good wishes,
there's the new frock I've been dieting into for
more than a fortnight
quite intact
over the back of the chair.
And because last night was my last night,
last night I left you,
left you to your own devices under the double duvet
and went home to home-home
to sleep my last night in my own
single bed.
I'd love to say I've my own
old toys around me, et cetera and the same old old-

gold counterpane, but is it likely?
Is it likely what with the old dear's passion
for continuous redecoration,
there's not so much as a Sundayschool prize
not long gone to Oxfam –
just one wall-eyed
teddybear some rugby player gave me for my
twentyfirst
and an acrylic still life with aubergine
(which for one moment I consider asking for –
except where could we hang it?)
to take home to our home, our
old home which today's nuptials must make
our new home,
take home to remind myself of what I can't remember
which is what the hell the girl who did that picture
and was as far as I can remember
painting-daft
has to do with me,
the me with the Lanchester look.

Breakfast.
Breakfast on a tray and like a
condemned man I
can have anything I want for
breakfast, but
before I can lop the top off my boiled egg,
before I can say soldiers far less
dunk them, the place is
bristling with sisters
stripping me and unzipping me
and down the hall the bathroom taps are pounding
Niagara and bubbles.
'Buck's Fizz three fingers cheers kiddo cheerio'
this is Ellen

the older one
the matron of honour
clashing glasses knocking it back
in her slip and stocking soles
plugging in her Carmens
drenching herself in the Dutyfree Diorissimo
Dave brought back from that refresher course in
Brussels with his secretary
unpacking Mothercare plastic carriers
of maximum security sanitary protection from
her Antler overnight case because
she never knows the minute
with that new coil she had fitted after Timothy.
And Susan,
our Susan,
sixteen, sly eyes and skinny as a wand, she's
always fancied you,
ecru and peach, apple green satin, she'll
take all the eyes even though it's meant to be
My Day,
the bizzum's in kinks over the under-
crotch buttons of my camiknickers and I'm
to touch nothing till that
Hazel comes to comb out my hair.

Mother is being very mother-
of-the-bride, rushing round squeezing
Euthymol-pink shrimp-flavoured creamcheese
on platters of crackers bigger than millwheels
and though her daughters all agree
a donkey-brown twopiece is somewhat
less than festive
at least we're all thankful she's not
drawing squinty seams up the back of her legs
with eyebrow pencil

in memory of her wedding
in nineteen forty-three.

And here's the taxi
and I stretch up my arms
like one beseeching heaven
like one embracing fate
and four sets of hands help me into my dress
my dress I don't want to wear
my dress that after the whole kerfuffle
is really nothing special
my dress that, should you jilt me
leave me in the lurch at the altar of the registry office
tilting my
fragile psyche
for ever permanently agley,
the dress I'll have to wear for ever
till I'm dafter than Miss Havisham
in mourning for my life until it rots under the oxters.
I should have
chosen really carefully.

And then with Dad in the taxi
and I know
it's going to crash because there's got to be
something
going to stop me from ruining my life like this
but no,
no Dad winks and one swig
from his hipflask and we're bowling
gaily down the aisle towards you,
you and the best man I've been
knocking off for yonks
with his grin
and the ring
and his pockets
bulging obscenely with apocryphal telegrams.

Because we have opted for a
Quiet Wedding
and a civil sort of civil ceremony
the front four pews are chockablock with
all our old lovers
who (since we've taken
so long to tie the knot) have all been
married to each other, separated, been
divorced so long
they're on really friendly terms again and
surely someone,
someone will declare some
just impediment to stop this whole ridiculous
charade?
I make my vows
but all the time I'm screaming
'No No No' I
hear a voice
a voice I'm sure I recognize to be my own voice
loud as you like 'I do'.

Despite
the unfortunate business at the
Reception and the
manageress's Jack Russell
depositing that dead rat right at my satin slippers
under the top table while
(animal lovers to a man) the company
applauded laughed and cheered –
despite
the fact that when we came to cut the cake
it collapsed
like a prizewinning office block
in a spectacular shambles of silver

cardboard Ionic columns and white
plasterboard icing sugar we got
into the going away car while the going
was good and now,
now here we are
alone at last
in the plumbed-in twin-
bedded room of this hotel
where we told the man we'd booked a double
but he smiled shrugged said
he'd no record of that and this was all they had
so take it or leave it.
So we did.

We unpack
our paperbacks. We
scorn such sentiments such institutionalizing as
making love on this our wedding night
and it's only
after (sudden lust
having picked us up by the scruff of the neck and
chucked us into
that familiar whirlpool) and
practised and perfect
we judder totally together
into amazed and wide-eyed calm and
I lie beside you
utterly content that I know for sure
that this is never
ever going to
work.

THE FURIES

I HARRIDAN

Mad Meg on my mantelpiece,
Dulle Griet by Bruegel, a Flemish masterpiece
in anybody's eyes. 'Well worth historical consideration'
was how I looked at it. The surrealist tradition
from Bosch to Magritte is such a Flemish thing!
Oh a work of great power, most interesting . . .
I chose it for my History of Art essay, took pains
to enumerate the monsters, reduce it all to picture planes.
I was scholarly, drew parallels
between Hieronymus Bosch's and Pieter Bruegel's Hells;
Compared and contrasted
Symbolism and Realism in the Flemish School;
discussed: Was Meg 'mad' or more Shakespearean Fool?

The fool I was! Mad Meg, Sour-Tongued Margot,
maddened slut in this mass of misery, a Virago,
at her wit's end, running past Hell's Mouth, all reason gone,
she has one mailed glove, one battered breastplate on.
Oh that kitchen knife, that helmet, that silent shout,
I know Meg from the inside out.

All she owns in one arm, that lost look in her eyes.
These days I more than sympathize.

Oh I am wild-eyed, unkempt, hellbent, a harridan.
My sharp tongue will shrivel any man.
Should our paths cross
I'll embarrass you with public tears, accuse you with my loss.

II SPINSTER

This is no way to go on.
Get wise. Accept. Be
a spinster of this parish.
My life's in shards.
I will keep fit in leotards.

Go vegetarian. Accept.
Support good causes.
Be frugal, circumspect.
Keep cats. Take tidy fits.
Go to evening classes.
Keep a nest-egg in the bank.
Try Yoga. Cut your losses.
Accept. Admit you're a bit of a crank –

Oh I may be a bit of a crank
but still I get by, frugally. Think positive.
I live and let live. Depend
on nobody. Accept.
Go in for self-improvement.
Keep up with trends.
I'll cultivate my conversation.
I'll cultivate my friends.
I'll grow a herbaceous border.
By hook by crook I'll get my house in order.

III BAWD

I'll get all dolled up in my gladrags, stay
up till all hours, oh
up to no good.

It'll amaze you, the company I keep –
and I'll keep them at arm's length –
I've hauled my heart in off my sleeve.

I'll let my hair down,
go blonde, be a bombshell, be on the make,
I'll gold-dig, I'll be frankly fake.

I'll paint my face up, paint the town,
have carmine nails, oh
be a fatal dame.
I've gold eyes, kohl sockets.
I'll look daggers, kill.
My lipstick colour's Merry Hell.

I'd frighten the French.
I'll be a torment, haunt men's dreams,
I'll wear my stockings black with seams.

I'll rouge my cleavage, flaunt myself, my heels
will be perilously high, oh
but I won't sway.
I'll shrug everything off the shoulder,
make wisecracks, be witty off the cuff.
Tell blue jokes in mixed company.

I'll be a bad lot.
I've a brass neck. There is mayhem in my smile.
No one will guess it's not my style.

The Mother

is always two-faced.
At best, she wished you
into being. Yes, it was she
cried at the seven drops of blood that fell,
staining the snow – she
who bargained crazily with Fate
for that longawaited child
as red as blood
as white as snow
and when you came true it was
she who clapped her hands merrily because
she was as happy as a Queen could be.
But she's always dying early,
so often it begins to look deliberate,
abandoning you,
leaving you to the terrible mercy
of the Worst Mother, the one who married your father.
She doesn't like you, she
prefers all your sisters, she
loves her sons.
She's jealous of mirrors.
She wants your heart in a casket.
When she cuts the apple in two and selflessly
takes the sour green half
she's good and glad to see you poisoned
by the sweet red pulp.
Tell me,
what kind of prudent parent
would send a little child on a foolish errand in the forest
with a basket jammed with goodies
and wolf-bait? Don't trust her an inch.

My Rival's House

is peopled with many surfaces.
Ormolu and gilt, slipper satin,
lush velvet couches,
cushions so stiff you can't sink in.
Tables polished clear enough to see distortions in.

We take our shoes off at her door,
shuffle stocking-soled, tiptoe – the parquet floor
is beautiful and its surface must
be protected. Dust
cover, drawn shade,
won't let the surface colour fade.

Silver sugar-tongs and silver salver,
my rival serves us tea.
She glosses over him and me.
I am all edges, a surface, a shell
and yet my rival thinks she means me well.
But what squirms beneath her surface I can tell.
Soon, my rival
capped tooth, polished nail
will fight, fight foul for her survival.
Deferential, daughterly, I sip
and thank her nicely for each bitter cup.

And I have much to thank her for.
This son she bore –
first blood to her –
never, never can escape scot free
the sour potluck of family.
And oh how close
this family that furnishes my rival's place.

Lady of the house.
Queen bee.
She is far more unconscious,
far more dangerous than me.
Listen, I was always my own worst enemy.
She has taken even this from me.

She dishes up her dreams for breakfast.
Dinner, and her salt tears pepper our soup.
She won't
give up.

The Other Woman

The other woman
lies
between us like a bolster.
When I hit out wild she's
insubstantial a
flurry of feathers a mere
sneezing irritant.
When my shaped and hardened words turn
machine-gun
against you she's rock solid
the sandbag you hide behind.

The other woman
lies
when she says she does not want
your guts for her garterbelt.
I send out spies, they say relax
she's a hag she's just a kid
she's not a patch she's nothing to she's
no oil painting.
I'd know her anywhere.
I look for her in department stores, I scan
every cinema-queue.
Sometimes suddenly in some downtown restaurant
I catch her eye
casting crazily around for me.

The other woman
lies
the other side of my very own mirror.
Sweet, when I smile
straight out for you, she

puts a little twist on it, my
right hand never knows what her left is doing.
She's sinister.
She does not mean you well.

The Hickie

I mouth
sorry in the mirror when I see
the mark I must have made just now
loving you.
Easy to say it's all right
adultery
like blasphemy is for believers but
even in our
situation simple etiquette says
love should leave us both unmarked.
You are on loan to me like a library book
and we both know it.
Fine if you love both of us
but neither of us must too much show it.

In my misted mirror
you trace two toothprints
on the skin of your shoulder and sure
you're almost quick enough
to smile out bright and clear for me
as if it was OK.

Friends again, together in this bathroom
we finish washing love away.

Song of Solomon

You
smell nice he said
what is it?
Honey? He nuzzled a soap-trace
in the hollow of her collarbone.
The herbs of her hair?
Salt? He licked
a riverbed between her breasts.

(He'd seemed
not unconvinced by the chemical
attar of roses at her armpit. She tried
to relax have absolute faith in
the expensive secretions of teased civet to
trust the musk at her pulse spots
never think of the whiff of
sourmilk from her navel
the curds of cheese between the toes
the dried blood smell of many small wounds
the stink of fish at her crotch.)

No there he was above her apparently
as happy as a hog rooting for truffles.
She caressed him behind the ear
with the garlic of her cooking-thumb.
She banged shut her eyes
and hoped he would not smell her fear.

Smuggler

For Susan Musgrave

Why she loved him, she said, was for
his black pirate's heart.
Get her, adrift in his
brass bed, half seas over, stared awake
by the matchbox she found last night
balanced on the bed head.
Contents: one single scarlet fingernail.

Love?
She explains it another way.
In a heatwave between the wars,
her maiden aunt once told her,
high in the Campsies (they had cycled
from Glasgow, they were fourteen, with
packed lunches in the baskets between the horns
of their handlebars) they skinnydipped and sunbathed
naked, she and her sister, and she slept.
She woke up later to a cloud and a bird like
a hawk circling and Nettie, her sister, her twin,
the one who died of T.B. at the time of Munich,
leant over her and bit her nipple off.

She explains it another way.

What the Pool Said, On Midsummer's Day

I've led you by my garrulous banks, babbling
on and on till – drunk on air
and sure it's only water talking –
you come at last to my silence.
Listen, I'm dark
and still and deep enough.
Even this hottest gonging sun
on this longest day
can't white me out.
What are you waiting for?
I lie here, inviting, winking you in.

The woman was easy.
Like to like, I called her, she came.
In no time I had her
out of herself, slipping on my water-stockings,
leaning into, being cupped and clasped
in my green glass bra.
But it's you I want, and you know it, man.
I watch you, stripped, knee-deep
in my shallows, telling yourself
that what makes you gasp
and balls your gut
is not my coldness but your own fear.

– Your reasonable fear,
what's true in me admits it.
(Though deeper, oh
older than any reason.)
Yes, I could

drown you, you
could foul my depths, it's not
unheard of. What's fish
in me could make flesh of you,

my wet weeds against your thigh, it
could turn nasty.
I could have you
gulping fistfuls fighting yourself
back from me.

I get darker and darker, suck harder.
On-the-brink man, you
wish I'd flash and dazzle again.
You'd make a fetish of zazzing dragonflies?
You want I should zip myself up
with the kingfisher's flightpath, be beautiful?
I say no tricks. I say just trust,
I'll soak through your skin and
slake your thirst.

I watch. You clench,
clench and come into me.

Midsummer Night

Was that a donkey braying in my dream?
Couldn't make head or tail of it but
it hawhawed itself blue in the face
whatever it was. Still, Confusion's clearly
what's called for in any comedy worth worrying about.
That and Chance
which certainly seems to be
playing its part all right.
So we're laughing?
Get us, half enchanted and undecided
whether or not to give in to it,
wandering the wide woods on such a night like
the wrong pair of ill-met demi-
lovers we most likely are
in far too high a pollen count for
anybody's comfort. This is the
silly season though – you said so yourself –
surely a solstice is a time for going to extremes.
Have a heart though, I've always been
the equinox sort – white nights
and talking till birdsong
are as new a taste to me as the
piny retsina we sat late in the restaurant with,
till one. And still no real dark yet
to go home in.

Earlier, between
the World Cup and Wimbledon the blue
TV lights flickered from every douce house
in the solid suburbs we drove through to come
to such a shifting place.

Remember the horses,
how silently they moved
from dark woods.
'Would you call this a green glade?' you
asking gravely with a glint,
the lilac haze and three rooks on the long meadow,
that russet shape that changed
we could swear it, and stretched
and lengthened to a fox and back to prick-eared
hare again. Nothing tonight could decide
what form to take.

We are good and strange to one another and no mistake.

Fetch on the First of January

Nae time eftir the Bells, and the
New Year new in wi' the
usual crowd, wi' whisky, cheers and kisses –
Ah'd aboot managed the windaes shut
some clown had thrown wide
hopin' tae hear the hooters on the Clyde
when the door went.
                Well, well,
who'd've thought Ah'd be staunin' there
tae first foot masel'?

This some kinnuffa Huntigowk for Hogmany?
Hell-mend-ye, ye're
a bad penny, Jimmy –
Mister Ne'erdy Ne'er-do-Weel
sae chitterin' ill-clad for the caul'
sae drawn an' pale,
oh, wi' the black bun burnin' a hole
in yir poackit an' the coal
a Live Coal.

'Gawn, get' – Ah should shout it,
should shake a stick or ma fist,
oh, but Ah should hunt ye, by Christ,
they wey you chased that big black tyke
that dogged ye wance, mind,
a' the way fae Hope Street, hame?

Ah'll no let ye near me,
don't make me laugh,
got a much better
Better Half.

Och, aye tae glower at each other
was tae keek in a gey distortin' mirror,
yet ye've the neck to come back again
wi yir bare face, Jake Fetch,
the image o' my ain.
Ice roon yir mooth when ye kiss me,
the cauld plumes o' yir breath,
Ah'm lukkin' daggers,
You're lukkin' like Death.
Ah'm damned if ye'll get past ma door,
nae fear!

Come away in, stranger, Happy New Year.

Mirror's Song

For Sally Potter

Smash me looking-glass glass
coffin, the one
that keeps your best black self on ice.
Smash me, she'll smash back –
without you she can't lift a finger.
Smash me, she'll whirl out like Kali,
trashing the alligator mantrap handbags
with her righteous karate.
The ashcan for the stubbed lipsticks
and the lipsticked butts,
the wet lettuce of fivers.
She'll spill the Kleenex blossoms,
the tissues of lies, the matted
nests of hair from the brushes'
hedgehog spikes, she'll junk
the dead mice and the tampons
the twinkling single eyes
of winkled out diamanté, the hatpins,
the whalebone and lycra,
the appleblossom and the underwires,
the chafing iron that kept them maiden,
the Valium and initialled hankies,
the lovepulps and the Librium,
the permanents and panstick and
Coty and Tangee Indelible,
Thalidomide and junk jewellery.

Smash me for your daughters and dead
mothers, for the widowed
spinsters of the first and every war –
let her

rip up the appointment cards for the
terrible clinics,
the Greenham summonses, that date
they've handed us. Let her rip.
She'll crumple all the
tracts and the adverts, shred
all the wedding dresses, snap
all the spike-heel icicles
in the cave she will claw out of –
a woman giving birth to herself.

Poem for Other Poor Fools

Since you went I've only cried twice.
Oh never over you. Once
it was an old head at a bus window
and a waving hand.
Someone's granny, a careful clutcher of her handbag
and wearing a rainhat despite the fact
it wasn't raining. Yet
waving, waving to grandchildren already turned away
engrossed in sweets she had left them.
Old head. Waving hand.

    Oh she wasn't the type to expose herself
    to the vagaries of weather
    (a rainhat in no rain)
    Yet waving, waving to those who had already
      turned away.

Then once it was a beggar by the pub doorway
and his naked foot.
Some drunk old tramp,
player of an out of tune mouthorgan
and begging. Instead of his cap,
his boot for alms.
His playing was hopeless,
his foot bare in the gutter in the rain,
his big boot before him, empty, begging.
Oh it was a scream. I laughed
and laughed till I cried.

It was just his poor
pink and purple naked foot
                                out on a limb
exposed.
And how (his empty boot) he got nothing in return.

Neckties

Paisleys squirm with spermatozoa.
All yang, no yin. Liberties are peacocks.
Old school types still hide behind their prison bars.
Red braces, jacquards, watermarked brocades
are the most fun a chap can have
in a sober suit.

You know about knots,
could tie, I bet, a bowtie properly
in the dark with your eyes shut, but
we've a diagram hung up
beside the mirror in our bedroom.
Left over right, et cetera . . .
The half or double Windsor,
even that extra fancy one it takes
an extra long tie to pull off successfully.
You know the times a simple schoolboy four-in-hand
will be what's wanted.

I didn't used to be married.
Once neckties were coiled occasional serpents
on the dressing-table by my bed
beside the car-keys and the teetering
temporary leaning towers of change.
They were dangerous nooses on the backs of chairs
or funny fishes in the debris on the floor.
I should have known better.

Picture me away from you
cruising the high streets
under the watchful eyes of shopboys
fingering their limp silks

wondering what would please you.
Watch out, someday I'll bring you back a naked lady,
a painted kipper, maybe a bootlace
dangling from a silver dollar
and matching collarpoints.
You could get away with anything
you're that goodlooking.
Did you like that screenprinted slimjim from Covent
    Garden?

Once I got a beauty in a Cancer Shop
and a sort of forties effort in Oxfam for a song.
Not bad for one dull town.
The dead man's gravy stain wasn't the size of sixpence
and you can hide it behind your crocodile tie pin.

The Redneck

The day I got married I was like a rake.
Six month on the popcorn diet. Starving
but I wouldn't give the girls at work the satisfaction.
All so as I could swan down the aisle in my Scarlet O'Hara
towards that pig with a knife stuck down his sock.
Kilt suited him, but. Unlike ma da.
A toss-up between the Ancient Buchanan
and the Hunting MacIntyre.
I wanted tartan yes but no too roary.
State I was in everything had to be just so.
I had my mammy roasted in a pinwheel hat.
Ended up whole thing was nothing but a blur
and him shouting 'Perfect Working Order'
every two minutes mooning his mates
and flashing the photographer with his
Lion Rampant boxer shorts. A right rid neck.

During my marriage I ballooned.
None of a family thank God.
Bad enough splitting up without the complications.

Inter-City

Hammered like a bolt
diagonally through Scotland (my
small dark country) this
train's a
swaying caveful of half-
seas over oil-men (fuck
this fuck that fuck
everything) bound for Aberdeen and
North Sea Crude.
Empty beercans of
spun aluminium roll like ballbearings
underfoot and
sloshing amber's a
storm in a whisky glass or two.
Outside's all
black absolutely
but for fizzing starbursts
of weirdblue or orange streetlights
and lit-up grids of windows.
Only bits of my own blurred
back-to-front face and
my mind elsewhere.
The artsyfartsy magazine I'm
not even pretending to read
wide open
at a photograph called Portrait of Absence.

The Bargain

The river in January is fast and high.
You and I
are off to the Barrows.
Gathering police-horses twitch and fret
at the Tron end of London Road and Gallowgate.
The early kick-off we forgot
has us, three thirty, rubbing the wrong way
against all the ugly losers
getting ready to let fly
where the two rivers meet.

January, and we're
looking back, looking forward,
don't know which way

but the boy
with three beautiful Bakelite
Bush radios for sale in Meadow's Minimarket is
buttonpopping stationhopping he
don't miss a beat   sings along   it's easy
to every changing tune.

Yes today we're in love aren't we?
with the whole splintering city
its big quick river   wintry bridges
its brazen black Victorian heart.
So what if every other tenement
wears its hearth on its gable end
all I want
is my glad eye to catch
a glint in your flinty Northern face again
just once. Oh I know it's cold

and coming down
and no we never lingered long among
the Shipbank traders.
Paddy's market   underneath the arches
stank too much today
the usual wetdog reek rising
from piles of old damp clothes.

Somebody absolutely steamboats he says on
sweet warm wine
swigged plaincover from a paper bag
squats in a puddle with nothing to sell
but three bent forks   a torn
calendar (last year's)
and a broken plastic sandal.
So we hadn't the stomach for it today.
We don't deserve a bargain then!
No connoisseur can afford to be too scrupulous
about keeping his hands clean.
There was no doubt   the rare   the beautiful
and the bugle beaded   the real antique   dirt cheap
among the rags and drunks
you could easily take to the cleaners.

At the Barrows everything has its price
no haggling   believe me
this boy knows his radios.
Pure utility
and what that's worth these days.
Suddenly the fifties are fashionable
and anything within a decade of art deco
a rarity you'll pay through the nose for.
The man with the patter and all these curtain lengths
in fibreglass is flabbergasted at the bargain
and says so in so many words.
Jesus, every other

arcade around here's
a 'Fire Surround Boutique' –
and we watch the struggling families;
father carrying hearth home
mother wound up with kids.
All the couples we know fall apart
or have kids.
Oh we've never shouldered much.
We'll stick to small ikons for our home –
as long as they're portable –
a dartboard   a peacock feather
a stucco photoframe.

We queue in a blue haze of hot fat
for Danny's Do-Nuts that grit
our teeth with granules of sugar.
I keep
losing you and finding you –
two stalls away you thumb
through a complete set of manuals for
primary teachers in the thirties.
I rub my sleeve
on a dusty Chinese saucer
till the gilt shows through.
Oh come on   we promised
we'd not let our affection for the slightly cracked
trap us into such expenditure again.
Oh even if it is a bargain
we won't buy.
The stallholder says we'll be the death of her
she says   see January
it's been the doldrums the day.

And it's packing up time
with the dark coming early
and as cold as the river.
By the bus stop I show you
the beady bag and the maybe rosewood box
with the inlaid butterfly and the broken catch.

You've bought a record by the Shangri-las
a pin-stripe waistcoat that needs a stitch
it just won't get   and a book called 'Enquire
Within – Upon Everything'.

The raw cold gets colder.
There doesn't seem to be a lot to say.
I wish we could either mend things
or learn to throw them away.

Hafiz on Danforth Avenue

There are no nightingales in this lunchroom, but
I have all these presents wrapped in that cheap
Christmas paper printed with those cardinals
you said sang out too loud.
Waiting for the
last of the breakfast specials I fish out
from the bottom of my handbag your father's
copy of Hafiz you lent me. Old ink
on the flyleaf, the name
that is also your name, the date
and where he bought it.

No place
for a lady here at eleven a.m.
in bitter mid December on the Danforth – all these
Greek men at the counter
on their rooted stools, sallow
under astrakhan, brindled moustaches,
the clack of worrybeads, I catch
a flash of amber and tassels.
A toothpick, a gold filling –
'Tonight I gonna finish one gallon of wine.
Tony makes it great. Forget
the mortgages, the pressure, tonight
if my wife she drives me I can get loaded.'

'A laughing winecup, a tangle
of knotted hair.' I tingle
remembering us side by side – I am reading
your old Hafiz, you the New Divan I
brought with me, somehow linking

Glasgow to Toronto to Teheran.
Later you stretch out,
the book is closed on the carpet,
a spiral of tangerine peel on the cover.

In the photograph you showed me Sunday
you are twelve, it is the year
you lived in Baghdad, you
are jug-eared, a proper cropped
North American boy.
There are two Iraqi taxidrivers,
a big Yankee car with
dangling charms of Islam. I can
smell the heat and the petrol.

'The morning breeze is the messenger of Love . . .
The Beloved
is sometimes the seller of sweetmeats,
the poet an eloquent sugarloving parrot.'
And today's snowflakes
muffle the mounds of Best Canadian
pumpkins and hubbardsquash outside
next door's greengrocery.
Here, through chromium and steam
the sugar dredger, a plate of lemons,
jellies, sherbet-coloured wedges
of chiffon pie.

The beautiful black waitress
wears a white beanie.

They've written Merry Christmas with glitterdust
on the mirror here in Motorama
beside the poster which says
Cold, Beautiful
Milk.

The young lovers
holding hands under the next table
play on the jukebox
'You don't bring me flowers'.

And to tell you this is easy,
scribbling this was as simple
as the shopping-list it jostles
on the next page of my notebook.
Love, as well as bread and coffee
it says eggplants, olive oil
don't forget
the nutmeg and cinnamon.

BERLIN POEMS

5TH APRIL 1990

Today I got back from Berlin and the broken Wall.
With bits of it.
Smithereens of history, the brittle confetti
of chiselled-off graffiti,
trickle on to the brave blue dogeared cover
of my signed copy of *Sonnets from Scotland*
that I had with me and have just unpacked.
It hasn't travelled well, but crumbled,
this souvenir I brought for Fünfzig Pfennige
picked out from the brightest chips,
from the priciest slabs with names
or obscenities half intact – all on offer
from that grinning gap-toothed Kreuzberg
Gastarbeiter kid who really thought
he had it made.
Well, he saw me coming all right –
another dumbcluck tourist
taking the slow curve of the Wall
towards Mariannenplatz, gawping at
the Bethanien-House artists mending
still-serviceable slogans on what was left standing.
This was a facelift the
chinking chisels of stonepeckers would
only worry at in turn and yet
they painted, and lovingly,
as if these fluorescents and enamels
would last one thousand years
and make good sense.
Every night I spent at Wannsee

at the Writers' House by the Lake,
Morgan's poems whirled me from space
to the bedrock of my own small
and multitudinous country, swung me
through centuries, ages, shifting geologies
till I was dizzy and dreamed
I was in the sands of the desert and the dead
as the poets lived it, just before my time,
then I was following Gerard Manley Hopkins
in priestly black up North Woodside Road
like a taunting Irish boy till I was suddenly,
stone cold sober, contemplating De Quincey
out of his mind in Rottenrow.

And all there was was
the symmetry of these turning pages,
fourteen lines mirroring fourteen lines,
the small circle of light
from the Bauhaus lamp on my borrowed desk
and the sough of trees in the Grunewald.

And outside there was Berlin.
The moneychangers at Zoostation
fanning out fistfuls of Ostmarks,
little lozenges of polystyrene, drifts and
spills from the packaging of dragged
video recorders and ghettoblasters,
blown white as hailstones and as light as popcorn
about their feet.
There was the wasted acreage of the Polish market
beside the Nationalgalerie where
the Ein' Mark, Ein' Mark, Ein' Mark
everything cost was so slow coming in
some of these sellers-in-hell bought
bottles of berry vodka from fellow blackmarketeers

with all they'd made and more, gave up,
got too blitzed to even pretend
to peddle bits of tractors, tools, laces,
mushrooms from polluted fields
bashed tins filched from hungry Warsaw,
bumpy Eastern European school shoes
to the haggling Turkish families from
the U-bahn's Istanbul Express.

And now I'm home
with three painted Polish Easter eggs,
Hungarian opera duets, Romanian symphonies,
an uncopyrighted East German Mickey Mouse
painted the wrong colours,
funny tasting chocolate
and the Rolling Stones 'in ctepeo'
Made in Bulgaria *Made in the Shade*.
And bits of the wall that are almost powder.
I think who could make sense of it?
Morgan could, yes Eddie could, he would.
And that makes me want to try.

AQUARIUM 1

in the fin-
de-siècle gloom
of the berlin aquarium
what little what thick
light we move through (so
slowly) is
underwater green.

lugubrious big fishes
in cross sections of small ponds
bump blunt noses
against their world's end.
there are razorbills, swords, pigsnouts, fronds,
metallics, micas, twists of tiffany glass —
impossible in this changed air to say
what's animal, or vegetable, or mineral.
louvred shoals flicker open shut off on
are gone.
one's a
tilted tin box
articulated awkwardly,
the next is a sinuous slip-of-a-thing
swivelling through tattered café curtains of bladderwrack
with a torchsinger's pout
to a bugeyed audience of
little fish who roll their eyes as if to say
get this
and gasp with just-too-regular-
to-not-be-phoney
openmouthed surprise.

things pulse
like hearts and lungs

in hard-to-look-at
medical programmes on your home aquarium
and anemones bloom and close
in fast photography through
day night day night day night day
five unshrivelling seasons every minute.
here are the lurid tentacles
of amazing latex nineteen-fifties
woolworth's swimming caps.
there is a real
Ripper's peasouper
encased in a green glass box
and in it
one obscene frill ripples.

and this, this
is neon graffiti
writing itself, wiping itself
on a wall of water.

AQUARIUM 2

everything
looks more alive
than a crocodile
even the
slimy reptilian turds
of the crocodiles
more likely to slither
or the lumps of terrible meat
nacreous with the iridescent
sickness of the pearl on their
cruel red stumps rejoin and walk
than this shrivelled elbow or
these claws engaged not a
splash or even a bubble in this
dire stink you cannot breathe in.
but the ragged long mouths
of the crocodiles and their various
species and snouts
are as indistinguishable and divers
as the sleeping hatred of europe
and you cannot tell what crocodiles
are made of any more than the
sleeping hatreds of europe
(whether bark or hide or barnacled stone
ancient and primeval and awful)
but these sleeping monuments
are alive and dangerous
as the sleeping hatreds of europe.

Everybody's Mother

Of course
everybody's mother always and
so on . . .

Always never
loved you enough
or too smothering much.

Of course you were the Only One, your
mother
a machine
that shat out siblings, listen

everybody's mother
was the original Frigid-
aire Icequeen clunking out
the hardstuff in nuggets, mirror-
silvers and ice-splinters that'd stick
in your heart.

Absolutely everyone's mother
was artistic when she was young.

Everyone's mother
was a perfumed presence with pearls, remote
white shoulders when she
bent over in her ball dress
to kiss you in your crib.

Everybody's mother slept with the butcher
for sausages to stuff you with.

Everyone's mother
mythologized herself. You got mixed up
between dragon's teeth and blackmarket stockings.

Naturally
she failed to give you
Positive Feelings
about your own sorry
sprouting body (it was a bloody shame)

but she did
sit up all night sewing sequins
on your carnival costume

so you would have a good time

and she spat
on the corner of her hanky and scraped
at your mouth with sour lace till you squirmed

so you would look smart

And where
was your father all this time?
Away
at the war, or
in his office, or any-
way conspicuous for his
Absence, so

what if your mother did
float around above you
big as a barrage balloon
blocking out the light?

Nobody's mother can't not never do nothing right.

Poem for My Sister

My little sister likes to try my shoes,
to strut in them,
admire her spindle-thin twelve-year-old legs
in this season's styles.
She says they fit her perfectly,
but wobbles
on their high heels, they're
hard to balance.

I like to watch my little sister
playing hopscotch, admire the neat hops-and-skips of her,
their quick peck,
never-missing their mark, not
over-stepping the line.
She is competent at peever.

I try to warn my little sister
about unsuitable shoes,
point out my own distorted feet, the calluses,
odd patches of hard skin.
I should not like to see her
in my shoes.
I wish she could stay
sure footed,
                    sensibly shod.

After the War

For Susanne Ehrhardt

After the war
was the dull country I was born in.
The night of Stafford Cripps's budget
My dad inhaled the blue haze of one last Capstan
then packed it in.
'*You were just months old . . .*'
The Berlin airlift.
ATS and REME badges
rattled in our button box.

Were they surprised that everything was different now?
Did it cheese them off that it was just the same
stuck in one room upstairs at my grandma's
jammed against the bars of my cot
with one mended featherstitch jumper drying
among the nappies on the winterdykes,
the puffed and married maroon counterpane
reflected in the swinging mirror of the wardrobe.
Radio plays. Them loving one another
biting pillows
in the dark while I was sleeping.
All the unmarried uncles were restless,
champing at the bit for New Zealand, The Black Country,
    Corby.
My aunties saved up for the New Look.

By International Refugee Year
we had a square green lawn and a twelve-inch tele.

1953

All the Dads, like you, that spring
had put the effort in.
Stepped on it with brand new spades
to slice and turn
clay-heavy wet yellow earth
to clods that stank of clay
and were well marbled
with worms and rubble.
You set paths straight
with slabs it took two men to lift.
Tipped barrowloads of topsoil. Riddled.
Sowed grass seed from illustrated packets
that showed tall flowers, long English lawns
striped green like marrows. Then
stretched over paper bowties on strings
to frighten birds.
So gardens happened
where the earth had been one raw wound.

And behind whitened windows
the Mums were stippling walls
or treadling Singers as they
ran rivers of curtain material
through the eye of a needle and out again,
fit to hang by Coronation Day.
This was in rooms
that had emptinesses, possibilities,
still smelled of shaved wood
and drying plaster.

In no time at all
in a neat estate a long time later
I will watch in a dawn
through a crack in drawn curtains
this lawn, the late September borders,
mature roses
and the undertaker coming up the path
carrying a pint of milk.

Sorting Through

The moment she died, my mother's dancedresses
turned from the colours they really were
to the colours I imagine them to be.
I can feel the weight of bumptoed silver shoes
swinging from their anklestraps as she swaggers
up the path towards *her* Dad, light-headed
from airman's kisses. Here, at what I'll have to learn
to call *my father's house*, yes every duster prints her
even more vivid than an Ilford snapshot on some seafront
in a white cardigan and that exact frock.
Old lipsticks. Liquid stockings.
Labels like *Harella, Gor-ray, Berketex.*
And, as I manhandle whole outfits into binbags for
   Oxfam,
every mote in my eye is a utility mark
and this is useful:
the sadness of dispossessed dresses,
the decency of good coats roundshouldered
in the darkness of wardrobes,
the gravitas of lapels,
the invisible danders of skin fizzing off from them
like all that life that will not neatly end.

Little Women

For Carol Ann Duffy and Jackie Kay

for that new girl Helen Derry
initially
I had everybody's fullest sympathy –
which entirely failed to comfort me.
That Helen Derry, yon one,
her with the wee fur cuffs on her bootees, the
knife edges on her accordion pleats which,
when she birled to swing them
in a quick scart along the peever beds
or bent to touch her toes, showed
a quick flash of her scut
in pants embroidered with the days of the week.
Rumour was she'd plain refused once to come to school
with Thursday on on a Monday and ever since –
oh, she was a hard case that Helen Derry –
her mother had learned her lesson, taken
a tumble to herself, got a grip and shaped up
good and proper.

My mother was predictable.
If that was the kind of friend Oona was, well,
she was no friend of mine, good riddance.
She was somebody anybody,
anybody with a bit of sense,
would be glad to see the back of.
Which was, wasn't it, just what a mother *would* say?
And everybody in the class said the novelty would wear off.
'Bide your time' and 'She'll come running back'
these seemed to be the bromides of conventional wisdom.
And, Helen Derry, as for her, she could

get back to where they called Levoy 'Bendulum'
(Bendulum!)
and Dutch ropes 'French' and she could just
take her wee blue bottle of Evening-in-bloody-Paris
back with her, coming here breaking up the
true marriage of a best friendship
with her face like the back of a bus
and her bahookey like the side of a house
and the wings on the famous specs you couldn't get on the
    NHS
and the 'auntie an airhostess'
and the wee lucky birthstone pierced earrings, the monster.

But I knew everybody knew what I knew.
There was something wrong with what I'd had with Oona.
Although the sanctity of our togetherness had seemed unbroken
and her content – I'd thought – to swap scraps
with no thought of anyone else or anything 'missing' –
us able to run the gauntlet of a three-legged race in perfect step
    together
with hardly a knot in the hanky that yoked us together
Now I was bad luck, bad luck altogether.
No wonder all the other couples avoided me,
frantically spooling themselves into each other tightly
with loving lassos of the french-knitting that ravelled endlessly
from the wee dolly-things that were all the craze
and they worried at like rosaries.
'There but for the Grace of God' and
'Please, please let it never happen to me, so help me' –
seemed to be the size of it as they jumped double bumps
    together,
arms down each other's coatsleeves, and chewed each other's
used bubble gum for luck and love.
What the magazines said was that this was a chance,
a chance to be truly honest with yourself

and see where you had gone wrong, or slipped up,
or let yourself go, or taken things for granted,
been lax about 'communicating' – for how many
of us could say we really took the time to talk or listen?
The magazines reminded that revenge
was a dish better eaten cold (and then you'd see it was only
good taste to leave it).

For Oona Cody's birthday – the first anniversary
since she'd left me – I bought her a copy of
Louisa May Alcott's two best-loved children's classics.
Yes. *Little Women* –
Little Women and *Good Wives* in a Compendium Edition
with a green marbled cover and one frontispiece,
a great book
I knew Oona – my Oona – would definitely love.
She was sitting under the pegs at playtime,
under the pegs with Helen Derry,
the both of them engrossed – or acting-it engrossed,
for God-knows-whose benefit though, so
(with hindsight) I'll concede it likely they *were* in
a mutual bona-fide brown study – engrossed
in a wee free-pamphlet entitled 'Growing Up'.
I clocked the cover (two doves and a butterfly
above the – open – gates of womanhood
with the pastel-coloured coloured-in country beyond).
And Oona Cody had the grace to blush
when I dropped the present – all wrapped up –
like a reproach in her lap.

I held my breath till lunchtime, when –
Helen Derry stood against the railings, watching –
Oona Cody marched up to me and said she didn't want a
    birthday present,
not from me, and anyway Helen had already read it.
'She says it's pure morbid, the wee sister dies

and the boy-next-door marries the wrong one,
the eejit that talks French and sleeps with
a clothespeg on her neb to improve her profile into aquiline
and thinks of nobody but herself and flaming art.'

So I had to go home with it,
home to face my mother's scorn,
to stick it up on the shelf beside the identical one I had already
knowing I'd never have the neck to take it back and swap it
for *What Katy Did & What Katy Did Next*
but was stuck with it –
'"*Christmas won't be Christmas without any presents,*" *grumbled Jo,*
    lying on the rug.'

Kidspoem/Bairnsang

It wis January
and a gey dreich day
the first day I went to the school
so
ma Mum happed me up in ma good navyblue nap coat
wi the rid tartan hood
birled a scarf aroon ma neck
pu'ed on ma pixie and ma pawkies
it wis that bitter
said
'noo ye'll no starve'
gied me a week kiss and a kidoan skelp on the bum
and sent me off across the playground
to the place I'd learn to say
'It was January
and a really dismal day
the first day I went to school
so
my Mother wrapped me up in my best navyblue top coat
with the red tartan hood
twirled a scarf around my neck
pulled on my bobble-hat and mittens
it was so bitterly cold
said
"now you won't freeze to death"
gave me a little kiss and a pretend slap on the bottom
and sent me off across the playground
to the place I'd learn to forget to say
"It wis January
and a gey dreich day
the first day I went to the school

so
ma Mum happed me up in ma good navyblue nap coat
wi the rid tartan hood
birled a scarf aroon ma neck
pu'ed on ma pixie and ma pawkies
it wis that bitter."'

Oh,
saying it was one thing
but when it came to writing it
in black and white
the way it had to be said
was as if
you were grown up, posh, male, English and dead.

Roger McGough

The Man in the Moon

On the edge of the jumping-off place I stood
Below me, the lake
Beyond that, the dark wood
And above, a night-sky that roared.

I picked a space between two stars
Held out my arms, and soared.

         *   *   *

The journey lasted not half a minute
There is a moon reflected in the lake
You will find me in it.

Defying Gravity

Gravity is one of the oldest tricks in the book.
Let go of the book and it abseils to the ground
As if, at the centre of the earth, spins a giant yo-yo
To which everything is attached by an invisible string.

Tear out a page of the book and make an aeroplane.
Launch it. For an instant it seems that you have fashioned
A shape that can outwit air, that has slipped the knot.
But no. The earth turns, the winch tightens, it is wound in.

One of my closest friends is, at the time of writing,
Attempting to defy gravity, and will surely succeed.
Eighteen months ago he was playing rugby,
Now, seven stones lighter, his wife carries him aw-

Kwardly from room to room. Arranges him gently
Upon the sofa for the visitors. 'How are things?'
Asks one, not wanting to know. Pause. 'Not too bad.'
(Open brackets. Condition inoperable. Close brackets.)

Soon now, the man that I love (not the armful of bones)
Will defy gravity. Freeing himself from the tackle
He will sidestep the opposition and streak down the wing
Towards a dimension as yet unimagined.

Back where the strings are attached there will be a service
And homage paid to the giant yo-yo. A box of left-overs
Will be lowered into a space on loan from the clay.
Then, weighted down, the living will walk wearily away.

Wearing Thin

'You'll soon grow into it,' she would say
When buying a school blazer three sizes too big.
And she was right as mothers usually are.

Syrup of figs. Virol. Cod liver oil.
Within a year I did grow into it
By then, of course, it was threadbare.

Pulling in different directions
My clothes and I never matched.
And in changing-rooms nothing has changed.

I can buy what I like and when
New clothes that are a perfect fit.
Full-length mirror, nervous grin,
It's me now that's threadbare, wearing thin.

A Joy to be Old

It's a joy to be old.
Kids through school,
The dog dead and the car sold.

Worth their weight in gold,
Bus passes. Let asses rule.
It's a joy to be old.

The library when it's cold.
Immune from ridicule.
The dog dead and the car sold.

Time now to be bold.
Skinnydipping in the pool.
It's a joy to be old.

Death cannot be cajoled.
No rewinding the spool.
The dog dead and the car sold.

Why do as you're told?
Have fun playing the fool.
It's a joy to be old.
The dog dead and the car sold.

Bits of Me

When people ask: 'How are you?'
I say, 'Bits of me are fine.'
And they are. Lots of me I'd take
anywhere. Be proud to show off.

But it's the bits that can't be seen
that worry. The boys in the backroom
who never get introduced.
The ones with the Latin names

who grumble about the hours I keep
and bang on the ceiling
when I'm enjoying myself. The overseers.
The smug biders of time.

Over the years our lifestyles
have become incompatible.
We were never really suited
and now I think they want out.

One day, on cue, they'll down tools.
Then it's curtains for me. (Washable
plastic on three sides.) Post-op.
Pre-med. The bed nearest the door.

Enter cheerful staff nurse (Irish
preferably), 'And how are you today?'
(I see red.) Famous last words:
'Bits of me are fine.' On cue, dead.

Crazy Bastard

I have always enjoyed the company of extroverts.
Wild-eyed men who would go too far
Up to the edge, and beyond. Mad, bad women.

Overcautious, me. Sensible shoes and a scarf
Tucked in. Fresh fruit and plenty of sleep.
If the sign said: 'Keep off', then off is where I'd keep.

*   *   *

Midsummer's eve in the sixties.
On a moonlit beach in Devon we sit around a fire
Drinking wine and cider. Someone strumming a guitar.

Suddenly, a girl strips off and runs into the sea.
Everybody follows suit, a whoop of flickering nakedness
Hot gold into cold silver   Far out.

Not wanting to be last in I unbutton my jeans.
Then pause. Someone had better stay behind
And keep an eye on the clothes. Common sense.

I throw another piece of driftwood on to the fire
Above the crackle listen to the screams and the laughter
Take a long untroubled swig of scrumpy. Crazy bastard.

Here I Am

Here I am
getting on for seventy
and never having gone to work in ladies' underwear

Never run naked at night in the rain
Made love to a girl I'd just met on a plane

At that awkward age now between birth and death
I think of all the outrages unperpetrated
opportunities missed

The dragons unchased
The maidens unkissed
The wines still untasted
The oceans uncrossed
The fantasies wasted
The mad urges lost

Here I am
as old as Methuselah
was when he was my age
and never having stepped outside for a fight

Crossed on red, pissed on rosé (or white)
Pretty dull for a poet, I suppose, eh? Quite.

Melting into the Foreground

Head down and it's into the hangover.
Last night was a night best forgotten.
(Did you really kiss a strange man on the forehead?)

At first you were fine.
Melting into the foreground.
Unassuming. A good listener.

But listeners are speakers
Gagged by shyness
And soon the wine has
Pushed its velvet fingers down your throat.

You should have left then. Got your coat.
But no. You had the Taste.
Your newfound gift of garbled tongue
Seemed far too good to waste.

Like a vacuum-cleaner on heat
You careered hither and thither
Sucking up the smithereens
Of half-digested chat.

When not providing the lulls in conversation
Your strangled banter
Stumbled on to disbelieving ears.

Girls braved your leering incoherences
Being too polite to mock
(Although your charm was halitoxic,
Your wit, wet sand in a sock).

When not fawning over the hostess
You were falling over the furniture
(Helped to your feet, I recall,
By the strange man with the forehead).

Gauche attempts to prise telephone numbers
From happily married ladies
Did not go unnoticed.

Nor did pocketing a bottle of Bacardi
When trying to leave
In the best coat you could find.

I'd lie low if I were you.
Stay at home for a year or two.
Take up painting. Do something ceramic.
Failing that, emigrate to somewhere Islamic.

The best of luck whatever you do.
I'm baling out, you're on your own.
Cockpit blazing, out of control,
Into the hangover. Head down.

Nothing Ventured

Nothing ventured
I rise from my hangover
And take a walk along the towpath.

The wind is acting plain silly
And the sky, having nobody to answer to
Is all over the place.

The Thames (as it likes to be called)
Gives a passable impersonation of a river
But I remain unimpressed.

Suddenly, in front of me, a woman.
We are walking at the same pace.
Lest she thinks I'm following her, I quicken mine.

She quickens hers. I break into a run.
So does she. It's looking bad now.
I'm gaining on her. God, what happens

When I catch up? Luckily, she trips
And sprawls headlong into a bed of nettles.
I sprint past with a cheery 'Hello'.

*   *   *

Out of sight, I leave the path and scramble
Down to the water's edge, where I lie down
And pretend to be a body washed ashore.

There is something very comforting
About being a corpse. My cares float away.
Like non-biodegradable bottles.

A cox crows, the crew slams on its oars
And a rowing-boat rises out of the water
To teeter on splintering legs like a drunken tsetse fly.

Before it can be disentangled
And reversed, a miracle; Lazarus risen
Is up and away along the towpath.

Near Hammersmith bridge, the trainer
Is on the other foot, as a hooded figure,
Face in shadow, comes pounding towards me.

A jogger? A mugger?
A mugger whose hobby is jogging? Vice versa?
(Why do such men always have 2 *g*'s?)

I search in vain for a bed of nettles. No need.
She sprints past with a cheery 'Hello'.
I recognize the aromatherapist from No. 75.

*   *   *

Waiting beneath the bridge for my breath
To catch up, I hear a cry. A figure is leaning
Out over the river, one hand on the rail.

His screaming is sucked into the slipstream
Of roaring traffic. On the walkway, pedestrians
Hurry past like bad Samaritans

I break into a sweat and a run
Simultaneously. 'Hold on,' I cry, 'Hold on.'
Galvanized, I am up the stairs and at his side.

The would-be suicide is a man in his late twenties.
His thin frame shuddering with despair.
His eyes, clenched tattoos — HATE   HATE.

My opening gambit is the tried and trusted
'Don't jump.' He walks straight into the cliché-trap.
'Leave me alone. I want to end it all.'

I ask him why? 'My wife has left me.'
My tone is sympathetic. 'That's sad,
But it's not the end of the world.'

'And I'm out of work and homeless.'
'It could be worse,' I say, and taking his arm
Firmly but reassuringly, move in close.

'If you think you're hard done by
You should hear what I've been through.
Suffering? I'll tell you about suffering.'

We are joined by a man in a blue uniform.
'I can handle this,' I snarl,
'You get back to your parking tickets.'

He turns out to be a Major
In the Salvation Army, so I relent
And let him share the intimacy of the moment.

I explain the loneliness that is forever
The fate of the true artist,
The icy coldness that grips the heart,

The black holes of infinite despair
Through which the sensitive spirit must pass,
The seasons in Hell, the flowers of evil.

*　　*　　*

The tide was turning and a full moon rising
As I lighted upon the existentialist nightmare:
The chaos within that gives birth to the dancing star.

I was illustrating the perpetual angst
And ennui with a recent poem
When the would-be suicide jumped. (First.)

The Sally Army officer, four stanzas later.
I had done my best. I cried my tears,
Crossed the road and headed west.

On the way home, needless to say, it rained.
My hangover welcomed me with open arms.
Nothing gained.

Ex Patria

After supper, we move out on to the veranda.
Moths flit between lamps. We drink, think about sex
and consider how best to wreck each other's lives.

At the river's edge, the kitchen maids are washing up.
In the age-old tradition, they slap the plates
against the side of a rock, singing tonelessly.

Like tiny chauffeurs, the mosquitoes will soon arrive
and drive us home. O England, how I miss you.
Ascot, Henley, Wimbledon. It's the little things.

The Map

Wandering lost and lonely in Bologna
I found a street-map on the piazza.
Unfortunately, it was of Verona.

As I was refolding it into a limp concertina,
A voice: 'Ah, you've found it! I'm Fiona,
Let me buy you a spritzer, over there on the terrazza.'

Two spritzers later we ordered some pasta
(Bolognese, of course, then zabaglione)
I felt no remorse, merely amore.

Proposing a toast to love at first sight,
We laughed and talked over a carafe of chianti
When out of the night, like a ghost, walked my aunty.

'Look who's here,' she cried. 'If it isn't our Tony,
Fancy bumping into you in Italy,
With a lady friend too,' then added bitterly:

'How are Lynda and the kids? I'm sure they're OK
While the mice are at home the tomcat will play.'
A nod to Fiona, 'Nice to meet you. Ciao!'

I snapped my grissini. 'Stupid old cow!'
Then turned to Fiona. She was no longer there.
Our romance in tatters, like the map on her chair.

It's Only a P . . .

Feeling a trifle smug after breaking off an untidy,
Drawn-out affair with somebody I no longer fancied
I was strolling through Kensington Gardens
When who should I bump into but Gavin.

Gavin, I should point out, is the husband.
'I'm worried about Lucy,' he said, straight out.
'I don't blame you,' I thought, but said nothing.
'I suspect she's having an affair. Any ideas?'

'Divorce,' I suggested. 'You might even get custody.'
'No, I mean Lucy,' he persisted. 'Who with?'
We walked on in silence, until casually, I asked:
'An affair, you say, what makes you so convinced?'

He stopped and produced from an inside pocket
A sheet of paper which I recognized at once.
It was this poem. Handwritten, an early draft.
Then I saw the gun. 'For God's sake, Gavin,
                                    It's only a p . . .

Your Favourite Hat

Believe me when I tell you that
I long to be your favourite hat

The velvet one. Purply-black
With ribbons trailing at the back

The one you wear to parties, plays,
Assignations on red-letter days

Like a bat in your unlit hall
I'd hang until there came the call

To freedom. To hug your crown
As you set off through Camden Town

To run my fingers through your hair
Unbeknown in Chalcot Square

To let them linger, let them trace
My shadow cast upon your face

Until, on reaching the appointed place
(The pulse at your temple, feel it race!)

Breathless, you whisper: 'At last, at last.'
And once inside, aside I'm cast

There to remain as time ticks by
Nap rising at each moan and sigh

Ecstatic, curling at the brim
To watch you naked, there with him

Until, too soon, the afternoon gone
You retrieve me, push me on

Then take your leave (as ever, in haste)
Me eager to devour the taste

Of your hair. Your temples now on fire
My tongue, the hatband as you perspire

To savour the dampness of your skin
As you window-gaze. Looking in

But not seeing. Over Primrose Hill
You dawdle, relaxed now, until

Home Sweet Home, where, safely back
Sighing, you impale me on the rack

Is it in spite or because of that
I long to be your favourite hat?

A Cautionary Calendar

Beware January,
His greeting is a grey chill.
Dark stranger. First in at the kill.
Get out while you can.

Beware February,
Jolly snowman. But beneath the snow
A grinning skeleton, a scarecrow.
Don't be drawn into that web.

Beware March,
Mad Piper in a many-coloured coat
Who will play a jig then rip your throat.
If you leave home, don't go far.

Beware April,
Who sucks eggs and tramples nests.
From the wind that molests
There is no escape.

Beware May,
Darling scalpel, gall and wormwood.
Scented blossom hides the smell
Of blood. Keep away.

Beware June,
Black lipstick, bruise-coloured rouge,
Sirensong and subterfuge.
The wide-eyed crazed hypnotic moon.

Beware July,
Its juices overflow. Lover of excess
Overripe in flyblown dress.
Insatiable and cruel.

Beware August,
The finger that will scorch and blind
Also beckons. The only place you will find
        To cool off is the morgue.

Beware September,
Who speaks softly with honeyed breath.
You promise fruitfulness. But death
        Is the only gift that she'll accept.

Beware October,
Whose scythe is keenest. The old crone
Makes the earth tremble and moan.
        She's mean and won't be mocked.

Beware November,
Whose teeth are sharpened on cemetery stones,
Who will trip you up and crunch your bones.
    Iron fist in iron glove.

Beware December,
False beard that hides a sneer.
Child-hater. In what year
        Will we know peace?

The End of Summer

It is the end of summer
The end of day and cool,
As children, holiday-sated,
Idle happily home from school.
Dusk is slow to gather
The pavements still are bright,
It is the end of summer
And a bag of dynamite

Is pushed behind the counter
Of a department store, and soon
A trembling hand will put an end
To an English afternoon.
The sun on rooftops gleaming
Underlines the need to kill,
It is the end of summer
And all is cool, and still.

When I am Dead

I could never begin a poem: 'When I am dead'
As several poets still alive have done.
The jokey Last Will, and litanies
Of things we are to do when they are gone.

Courageous stuff. Written I shouldn't wonder
The Morning After, in the throes
Of grim despair. Head still ringing from the noise
Of nights keeling over like glass dominoes.

The chill fear that perhaps the writer
Might outlive the verse, provides the spur
To nail the spectre down in print,
To risk a sort of atheistic prayer.

God, of course, does not appear in rhyme,
Poets of our time being more inclined
To dwell upon the price of manuscripts
And how they want the coffin lined.

Or ashes scattered, cats fed, ex-wives
Gunned down. Meanwhile, in a drawer
Neat and tidy, the bona fide Will,
Drawn-up and witnessed by an old family lawyer.

And though poets I admire have published poems
Whose imperfections reflect our own decay,
I could never begin a poem: 'When I am dead'
In case it tempted Fate, and Fate gave way.

The Trouble with Snowmen

'The trouble with snowmen,'
Said my father one year
'They are no sooner made
Than they just disappear.

I'll build you a snowman
And I'll build it to last
Add sand and cement
And then have it cast.

And so every winter,'
He went on to explain
'You shall have a snowman
Be it sunshine or rain.'

                *   *   *

And that snowman still stands
Though my father is gone
Out there in the garden
Like an unmarked gravestone.

Staring up at the house
Gross and misshapen
As if waiting for something
Bad to happen.

For as the years pass
And I grow older
When summers seem short
And winters colder

The snowmen I envy
As I watch children play
Are the ones that are made
And then fade away.

Hearts and Flowers

Aunty Marge,
Spinster of the parish, never had a boyfriend.
Never courted, never kissed.
A jerrybuilt dentist and a smashed jaw
Saw to that.

To her,
Life was a storm in a holy-water font
Across which she breezed
With all the grace and charm
Of a giraffe learning to windsurf.

But sweating
In the convent laundry, she would iron
Amices, albs and surplices
With such tenderness and care
You'd think priests were still inside.

Deep down,
She would like to have been a nun
And talked of missing her vocation
As if it were the last bus home:
'It passed me by when I was looking the other way.'

'Besides,'
She'd say, 'what Order would have me?
The Little Daughters of the Bingo?
The Holy Whist Sisters?' A glance at the ceiling.
'He's not that hard up.'

                              We'd laugh
And protest, knowing in our hearts that He wasn't.
But for the face she would have been out there,
Married, five kids, another on the way.
Celibacy a gift unearned, unasked for.

                              But though
A goose among grown-ups,
Let loose among kids
She was an exploding fireworks factory,
A runaway pantomime horse.

                              Everybody's
Favourite aunt. A cuddly toy adult
That sang loud and out of tune.
That dropped, knocked over and bumped into things,
That got ticked off just like us.

                              Next to
A game of cards she liked babysitting best.
Once the parents were out of the way
It was every child for itself. In charge,
Aunt Marge, renegade toddler-in-chief.

                              Falling
Asleep over pontoon, my sister and I,
Red-eyed, would beg to be taken to bed.
'Just one more game of snap,' she'd plead,
And magic two toffees from behind an ear.

Then suddenly
Whooshed upstairs in the time it takes
To open the front door. Leaving us to possum,
She'd tiptoe down with the fortnightly fib:
'Still fast asleep, not a murmur all night. Little angels.'

But angels
Unangelic, grew up and flew away. And fallen,
Looked for brighter toys. Each Christmas sent a card
With kisses, and wondered how she coped alone.
Up there in a council flat. No phone.

Her death
Was as quick as it was clumsy. Neighbours
Found the body, not us. Sitting there for days
Stiff in Sunday best. Coat half-buttoned, hat askew.
On her way to Mass. Late as usual.

Her rosary
Had snapped with the pain, the decades spilling,
Black beads trailing. The crucifix still
Clenched in her fist. Middle finger broken.
Branded into dead flesh, the sign of the cross.

From the missal
In her lap, holy pictures, like playing cards,
Lay scattered. Five were face-up:
A Full House of Sacred Hearts and Little Flowers.
Aunty Marge, lucky in cards.

Casablanca

You must remember this
To fall in love in Casablanca
To make it as a jockey in Morocco.

The size of tuppence
Photographs show Uncle Bill holding silver cups
Wearing sepia silks and a George Formby grin.

Dominique
Had silent film star looks. With brown eyes
Black hair and lips full to the brim, she was a race apart.

He brought her over
to meet the family early on. An exotic bloom
In bleak post-war Bootle. Just the once.

Had there been children
There might have been more contact. But letters,
Like silver cups, were few and far between.

At seventy-eight
It's still the same old story. Widowed and lonely.
The prodigal sold up and came back home.

I met him that first Christmas
He spoke in broken scouse. Apart from that
He looked like any other bowlegged pensioner.

He had forgotten the jockey part.
The fight for love and glory had been a brief episode
In a long, and seemingly, boring life.

It turned out
That he had never felt at home there.
Not a week went by without him thinking of Liverpool.

Casablanca
The airplane on the runway. She in his arms.
Fog rolling in from the Mersey. As time goes by.

Tramp Tramp Tramp

Insanity left him when he needed it most.
Forty years at Bryant & May, and a scroll
To prove it. Gold lettering, and a likeness
Of the Founder. Grandad's name writ small:
'William McGarry, faithful employee'.

A spent match by the time I knew him.
Choking on fish bones, talking to himself,
And walking round the block with a yardbrush
Over his shoulder. 'What for, Gran?' 'Hush . . .
Poor man, thinks he's marching off to war.

'Spitting image of Charlie, was your Grandad,
And taller too.' She'd sigh. 'Best-looking
Man in Seaforth. And straight-backed?
Why, he'd walk down Bridge Road
As if he had a coat-hanger in his suit.'

St Joseph's Hospice for the Dying
Is where Chaplin made his last movie.
He played Grandad, and gave a fine performance
Of a man raging against God, and cursing
The nuns and nurses who tried to hold him down.

Insanity left him when he needed it most.
The pillow taken from his face
At the moment of going under. Screaming
And fighting to regain the years denied,
His heart gave out, his mind gave in, he died.

The final scene brings tears to everybody's eyes.
In the parlour, among suppurating candles
And severed flowers, I see him smiling
Like I'd never seen him smile before.
Coat-hanger at his back. Marching off to war.

The Railings

You came to watch me playing cricket once.
Quite a few of the fathers did.
At ease, outside the pavilion
they would while away a Saturday afternoon.
Joke with the masters, urge on
their flannelled offspring. But not you.

Fielding deep near the boundary
I saw you through the railings.
You were embarrassed when I waved
and moved out of sight down the road.
When it was my turn to bowl though
I knew you'd still be watching.

Third ball, a wicket, and three more followed.
When we came in at the end of the innings
the other dads applauded and joined us for tea.
Of course, you had gone by then. Later,
you said you'd found yourself there by accident.
Just passing. Spotted me through the railings.

*   *   *

Speech-days · Prize-givings · School-plays
The Twentyfirst · The Wedding · The Christening
You would find yourself there by accident.
Just passing. Spotted me through the railings.

Squaring Up

When I was thirteen and crimping my first quiff
Dad bought me a pair of boxing-gloves
In the hope that I would aspire to the Noble Art.

But I knew my limitations from the start:
Myopia, cowardice and the will to come second.
But I feigned enthusiasm for his sake.

Straight after tea, every night for a week
We would go a few rounds in the yard.
Sleeves rolled-up, collarless and gloveless

He would bob and weave and leave me helpless.
Uppercuts would tap me on the chin
Left hooks muss my hair, haymakers tickle my ear.

Without gloves, only one thing was clear:
The fact that I was hopeless. He had a son
Who couldn't square up. So we came to blows.

Losing patience, he caught me on the nose.
I bled obligingly. A sop. A sacrifice.
Mum threw in the towel and I quit the ring.

But when the bell goes each birthday I still feel the sting
Not of pain, but of regret. You said sorry
And you were. I didn't. And I wasn't.

In at the Kill

The contractions are coming faster now.
Every ten minutes or so
A crush of pain made bearable
Only by the certainty of its passing.

Midwives come and go.
At nine forty-five, a show.
It must go on. The floodgates open,
A universe implodes.

There is no going back now
(As if there ever was). Shall I slip away
And start a new life?
Instead, I do as I am told:

'Push, push. Stop, stop. Now push.
Come on, more. The head's coming.
Push harder. Harder. Push, push.'
Then out it comes – whoosh.

Uncoiled, I am thrown back.
For some reason I twirl.
Doubledizzy, I steady myself
On the bedrail. 'It's a girl.'

                    *   *   *

And so it is. My first.
Having witnessed three sons bawl into view
With the familiar appendage of their gender,
I am unprepared for . . . (what's the word,

Begins with *p* and ends with *enda*?)
Amazed, not by any lack or absence
But by the prominence of the lack,
The perfect shape of the absence.

Flashbulbs interrupt my musing,
The theatre fills with flowers.
My wife leads the applause,
I bow. 'Thank you . . . Thank you . . .'

Cinders

After the pantomime, carrying you back to the car
On the coldest night of the year
My coat, black leather, cracking in the wind.

Through the darkness we are guided by a star
It is the one the Good Fairy gave you
You clutch it tightly, your magic wand.

And I clutch you tightly for fear you blow away
For fear you grow up too soon and – suddenly,
I almost slip, so take it steady down the hill.

Hunched against the wind and hobbling
I could be mistaken for your grandfather
And sensing this, I hold you tighter still.

Knowing that I will never see you dressed for the Ball
Be on hand to warn you against Prince Charmings
And the happy ever afters of pantomime.

On reaching the car I put you into the baby seat
And fumble with straps I have yet to master
Thinking, if only there were more time. More time.

You are crying now. Where is your wand?
Oh no. I can't face going back for it
Let some kid find it in tomorrow's snow.

Waiting in the wings, the witching hour.
Already the car is changing. Smells sweet
Of ripening seed. We must go. Must go.

Who are These Men?

Who are these men who would do you harm?
Not the mad-eyed who grumble at pavements
Banged up in a cell with childhood ghosts

Who shout suddenly and frighten you. Not they.
The men who would do you harm have gentle voices
Have practised their smiles in front of mirrors.

Disturbed as children, they are disturbed by them.
Obsessed. They wear kindness like a carapace
Day-dreaming up ways of cajoling you into the car.

Unattended, they are devices impatient
To explode. Ignore the helping hand
It will clench. Beware the lap, it is a trapdoor.

They are the spies in our midst. In the park,
Outside the playground, they watch and wait.
Given half a chance, love, they would take you

Undo you. Break you into a million pieces.
Perhaps, in time, I would learn forgiveness.
Perhaps, in time, I would kill one.

Just Passing

Just passing, I spot you through the railings.
You don't see me. Why should you?
Outside the gates, I am out of your orbit.

Break-time for Infants and first-year Juniors
and the playground is a microcosmos:
planets, asteroids, molecules, chromosomes.

Constellations swirling, a genetic whirlpool
Worlds within worlds. A Russian doll
of universes bursting at each seam.

Here and there, some semblance of order
as those who would benefit from rules
are already seeking to impose them.

Not yet having to make sense of it all
you are in tune with chaos, at its centre.
Third son lucky, at play, oblivious of railings.

I try and catch your eye. To no avail.
Wave goodbye anyway, and pocketing
my notebook, move on. Someday we must talk.

Bearhugs

Whenever my sons call round we hug each other.
Bearhugs. Both bigger than me and stronger
They lift me off my feet, crushing the life out of me.

They smell of oil paint and aftershave, of beer
Sometimes and tobacco, and of women
Whose memory they seem reluctant to wash away.

They haven't lived with me for years,
Since they were tiny, and so each visit
Is an assessment, a reassurance of love unspoken.

I look for some resemblance to my family.
Seize on an expression, a lifted eyebrow,
A tilt of the head, but cannot see myself.

Though like each other, they are not like me.
But I can see in them something of my father.
Uncles, home on leave during the war.

At three or four, I loved those straightbacked men
Towering above me, smiling and confident.
The whole world before them. Or so it seemed.

I look at my boys, slouched in armchairs
They have outgrown. See Tom in army uniform
And Finn in air force blue. Time is up.

Bearhugs. They lift me off my feet
And fifty years fall away. One son
After another, crushing the life into me.

Sharon Olds

Monarchs

All morning, as I sit thinking of you,
the Monarchs are passing. Seven storeys up,
to the left of the river, they are making their way
south, their wings the dark red of
your hands like butchers' hands, the raised
veins of their wings like your scars.
I could scarcely feel your massive rough
palms on me, your touch was so light,
the delicate chapped scrape of an insect's leg
across my breast. No one had ever
touched me before. I didn't know enough to
open my legs, but felt your thighs,
feathered with red-gold hairs,
      opening
between my legs
like a pair of wings.
The hinged print of my blood on your thighs –
a winged creature pinned there –
and then you left, as you were to leave
over and over, the butterflies moving
in masses past my window, floating
south to their transformation, crossing over
borders in the night, the diffuse blood-red
cloud of them, my body under yours,
the beauty and silence of the great migrations.

The Sisters of Sexual Treasure

As soon as my sister and I got out of our
mother's house, all we wanted to
do was fuck, obliterate
her tiny sparrow body and narrow
grasshopper legs. The men's bodies
were like our father's body! The massive
hocks, flanks, thighs, elegant
knees, long tapered calves –
we could have him there, the steep forbidden
buttocks, backs of the knees, the cock
in our mouth, ah the cock in our mouth.
                    Like explorers who
discover a lost city, we went
nuts with joy, undressed the men
slowly and carefully, as if
uncovering buried artefacts that
proved our theory of the lost culture:
that if Mother said it wasn't there,
it was there.

The Language of the Brag

I have wanted excellence in the knife-throw,
I have wanted to use my exceptionally strong and accurate
    arms
and my straight posture and quick electric muscles
to achieve something at the center of a crowd,
the blade piercing the bark deep,
the haft slowly and heavily vibrating like the cock.

I have wanted some epic use for my excellent body,
some heroism, some American achievement
beyond the ordinary for my extraordinary self,
magnetic and tensile, I have stood by the sandlot
and watched the boys play.

I have wanted courage, I have thought about fire
and the crossing of waterfalls, I have dragged around

my belly big with cowardice and safety,
my stool black with iron pills,
my huge breasts oozing mucus,
my legs swelling, my hands swelling,
my face swelling and darkening, my hair
falling out, my inner sex
stabbed again and again with terrible pain like a knife.
I have lain down.

I have lain down and sweated and shaken
and passed blood and feces and water and
slowly alone in the center of a circle I have
passed the new person out
and they have lifted the new person free of the act
and wiped the new person free of that
language of blood like praise all over the body.

I have done what you wanted to do, Walt Whitman,
Allen Ginsberg, I have done this thing,
I and the other women this exceptional
act with the exceptional heroic body,
this giving birth, this glistening verb,
and I am putting my proud American boast
right here with the others.

I Could Not Tell

I could not tell I had jumped off that bus,
that bus in motion, with my child in my arms,
because I did not know it. I believed my own story:
I had fallen, or the bus had started up
when I had one foot in the air.

I would not remember the tightening of my jaw,
the rage that I'd missed my stop, the leap
into the air, the clear child
gazing about her in the air as I plunged
to one knee on the street, scraped it, twisted it,
the bus skidding to a stop, the driver
jumping out, my daughter laughing
Do it again.

           I have never done it
again. I have been very careful.
I have kept an eye on that nice young mother
who suddenly threw herself
off the moving vehicle
onto the stopped street, her life
in her hands, her life's life in her hands.

Ideographs

A photograph of China, 1905

The small scaffolds, boards in the form of
ideographs, the size of a person,
lean against a steep wall
of dressed stone. One is the simple
shape of a man. The man on it
is asleep, his arms nailed to the wood.
No timber is wasted; his fingertips
curl in at the very end of the plank
as a child's hands open in sleep.
The other man is awake – he looks
directly at us. He is fixed to a more
complex scaffold, a diagonal cross-piece
pointing one arm up, one down,
and his legs are bent, the spikes through his ankles
holding them up off the ground,
his knees cocked, the folds of his robe flowing
sideways as if he were suspended in the air
in flight, his naked legs bared.
They are awaiting execution, tilted against the wall
as you'd prop up a tool until you needed it.
They'll be shouldered up over the crowd and
carried through the screaming. The sleeper will wake.
The twisted one will fly above the faces, his
garment rippling.
Here there is still the backstage quiet,
the dark at the bottom of the wall, the props
leaning in the grainy half-dusk.
He looks at us in the silence. He says
Save me, there is still time.

Race Riot, Tulsa, 1921

The blazing white shirts of the white men
are blanks on the page, looking at them is like
looking at the sun, you could go blind.
Under the snouts of the machine guns,
the dark glowing skin of the women and
men going to jail. You can look at the
gleaming horse-chestnuts of their faces the whole day.
All but one descend from the wood
back of the flat-bed truck. He lies,
shoes pointed North and South,
knuckles curled under on the splintered slats,
head thrown back as if he is in
a field, his face tilted up
toward the sky, to get the sun on it, to
darken it more and more toward the color of the human.

The Guild

Every night, as my grandfather sat
in the lampless room in front of the fire,
the liquor like fire in his hand, his eye
glittering meaninglessly in the light
from the flames, his glass eye baleful and stony,
a young man sat with him
in silence and darkness, a college boy
with white skin, unlined, a narrow
beautiful face, a broad domed
forehead, and eyes amber as the resin from
trees too young to be cut yet.
This was his son, who sat, an apprentice,
night after night, his glass of coals
next to the old man's glass of coals,
and he drank when the old man drank, and he learned
the craft of oblivion – that young man
not yet cruel, his dark hair as the
soil that feeds the tree's roots,
that son who would come to be in his turn
better at this than the teacher, the apprentice
who would pass his master in oblivion,
drinking steadily by the flames in the blackness,
that young man my father.

Miscarriage

When I was a month pregnant, the great
clots of blood appeared in the pale
green swaying water of the toilet.
Dark red like black in the salty
translucent brine, like forms of life
appearing, jelly-fish with the clear-cut
shapes of fungi.

That was the only appearance made
by that child, the dark, scalloped shapes
falling slowly. A month later
our son was conceived, and I never went back
to mourn the one who came as far as the
sill with its information: that we could
botch something, you and I. All wrapped in
purple it floated away, like a messenger
put to death for bearing bad news.

The Connoisseuse of Slugs

When I was a connoisseuse of slugs
I would part the ivy leaves, and look for the
naked jelly of those gold bodies,
translucent strangers glistening along
the stones, slowly, their gelatinous bodies
at my mercy. Made mostly of water, they would shrivel
to nothing if they were sprinkled with salt,
but I was not interested in that. What I liked
was to draw aside the ivy, breathe the
odor of the wall, and stand there in silence
until the slug forgot I was there
and sent its antennae up out of its
head, the glimmering umber horns
rising like telescopes, until finally the
sensitive knobs would pop out the ends,
delicate and intimate. Years later,
when I first saw a naked man,
I gasped with pleasure to see that quiet
mystery re-enacted, the slow
elegant being coming out of hiding and
gleaming in the dark air, eager and so
trusting you could weep.

New Mother

A week after our child was born,
you cornered me in the spare room
and we sank down on the bed.
You kissed me and kissed me, my milk undid its
burning slip-knot through my nipples,
soaking my shirt. All week I had smelled of milk,
fresh milk, sour. I began to throb:
my sex had been torn easily as cloth by the
crown of her head, I'd been cut with a knife and
sewn, the stitches pulling at my skin –
and the first time you're broken, you don't know
you'll be healed again, better than before.
I lay in fear and blood and milk
while you kissed and kissed me, your lips hot and swollen
as a teenage boy's, your sex dry and big,
all of you so tender, you hung over me,
over the nest of stitches, over the
splitting and tearing, with the patience of someone who
finds a wounded animal in the woods
and stays with it, not leaving its side
until it is whole, until it can run again.

Sex without Love

How do they do it, the ones who make love
without love? Beautiful as dancers,
gliding over each other like ice-skaters
over the ice, fingers hooked
inside each other's bodies, faces
red as steak, wine, wet as the
children at birth whose mothers are going to
give them away. How do they come to the
come to the   come to the   God   come to the
still waters, and not love
the one who came there with them, light
rising slowly as steam off their joined
skin? These are the true religious,
the purists, the pros, the ones who will not
accept a false Messiah, love the
priest instead of the God. They do not
mistake the lover for their own pleasure,
they are like great runners: they know they are alone
with the road surface, the cold, the wind,
the fit of their shoes, their overall cardio-
vascular health – just factors, like the partner
in the bed, and not the truth, which is
the single body alone in the universe
against its own best time.

Rite of Passage

As the guests arrive at our son's party
they gather in the living room —
short men, men in first grade
with smooth jaws and chins.
Hands in pockets, they stand around
jostling, jockeying for place, small fights
breaking out and calming. One says to another
How old are you? Six. I'm seven. So?
They eye each other, seeing themselves
tiny in the other's pupils. They clear their
throats a lot, a room of small bankers,
they fold their arms and frown. *I could beat you
up*, a seven says to a six,
the dark cake, round and heavy as a
turret, behind them on the table. My son,
freckles like specks of nutmeg on his cheeks,
chest narrow as the balsa keel of a
model boat, long hands
cool and thin as the day they guided him
out of me, speaks up as a host
for the sake of the group.
We could easily kill a two-year-old,
he says in his clear voice. The other
men agree, they clear their throats
like Generals, they relax and get down to
playing war, celebrating my son's life.

35/10

Brushing out our daughter's dark
silken hair before the mirror
I see the gray gleaming on my head,
the silver-haired servant behind her. Why is it
just as we begin to go
they begin to arrive, the fold in my neck
clarifying as the fine bones of her
hips sharpen? As my skin shows
its dry pitting, she opens like a small
pale flower on the tip of a cactus;
as my last chances to bear a child
are falling through my body, the duds among them,
her full purse of eggs, round and
firm as hard-boiled yolks, is about
to snap its clasp. I brush her tangled
fragrant hair at bedtime. It's an old
story – the oldest we have on our planet –
the story of replacement.

The Missing Boy

For Etan Patz

Every time we take the bus
my son sees the picture of the missing boy.
He looks at it like a mirror – the dark
blond hair, the pale skin,
the blue eyes, the electric-blue sneakers with
slashes of jagged gold. But of course
that kid is little, only six and a half,
an age when things can happen to you,
when you're not really safe, and our son is seven,
practically fully grown – why, he would
tower over that kid if they could
find him and bring him right here on this bus and
stand them together. He sways in the silence
wishing for that, the tape on the picture
gleaming over his head, beginning to
melt at the center and curl at the edges as it
ages. At night, when I put him to bed,
my son holds my hand tight
and says he's sure that kid's all right,
nothing to worry about, he just
hopes he's getting the food he likes,
not just any old food, but the food
he likes the most, the food he is used to.

Bestiary

Nostrils flared, ears pricked,
our son asks me if people can mate
with animals. I say it hardly
ever happens. He frowns, fur and
skin and hooves and slits and pricks and
teeth and tails whirling in his brain.
You *could* do it, he says, not wanting the
world to be closed to him in any
form. We talk about elephants
and parakeets, until we are rolling on the
floor, laughing like hyenas. Too late,
I remember love – I backtrack
and try to slip it in, but that is
not what he means. Seven years old,
he is into hydraulics, pulleys, doors which
fly open in the side of the body,
entrances, exits. Flushed, panting,
hot for physics, he thinks about lynxes,
eagles, pythons, mosquitoes, girls,
casting a glittering eye of use
over creation, wanting to know
exactly how the world was made to receive him.

The One Girl at the Boys' Party

When I take our girl to the swimming party
I set her down among the boys. They tower
and bristle, she stands there smooth and sleek,
her math scores unfolding in the air around her.
They will strip to their suits, her body hard and
indivisible as a prime number,
they'll plunge in the deep end, she'll subtract
her height from ten feet, divide it into
hundreds of gallons of water, the numbers
bouncing in her mind like molecules of chlorine
in the bright blue pool. When they climb out,
her ponytail will hang its pencil lead
down her back, her narrow silk suit
with hamburgers and french fries printed on it
will glisten in the brilliant air, and they will
see her sweet face, solemn and
sealed, a factor of one, and she will
see their eyes, two each,
their legs, two each, and the curves of their sexes,
one each, and in her head she'll be doing her
wild multiplying, as the drops
sparkle and fall to the power of a thousand from her body.

Summer Solstice, New York City

By the end of the longest day of the year he could not stand it,
he went up the iron stairs through the roof of the building
and over the soft, tarry surface
to the edge, put one leg over the complex green tin cornice
and said if they came a step closer that was it.
Then the huge machinery of the earth began to work for his
        life,
the cops came in their suits blue-gray as the sky on a cloudy
        evening,
and one put on a bullet-proof vest,
a black shell around his own life,
life of his children's father, in case
the man was armed, and one, slung with a
rope like the sign of his bounden duty,
came up out of a hole in the top of the neighboring building
like the gold hole they say is in the top of the head,
and began to lurk toward the man who wanted to die.
The tallest cop approached him directly,
softly, slowly, talking to him, talking, talking,
while the man's leg hung over the lip of the next world
and the crowd gathered in the street, silent, and the
hairy net with its implacable grid was
unfolded near the curb, and spread out, and
stretched as the sheet is prepared to receive at a birth.
Then they all came a little closer
where he squatted next to his death, his shirt
glowing its milky glow like something
growing in a dish at night in the dark in a lab and then
everything stopped
as his body jerked and he
stepped down from the parapet and went toward them

and they closed on him, I thought they were going to
beat him up, as a mother whose child has been
lost may scream at the child when it's found, they
took him by the arms and held him up and
leaned him against the wall of the chimney and the
tall cop lit a cigarette
in his own mouth, and gave it to him, and
then they all lit cigarettes, and the
red, glowing ends burned like the
tiny campfires we lit at night
back at the beginning of the world.

On the Subway

The young man and I face each other.
His feet are huge, in black sneakers
laced with white in a complex pattern like a
set of intentional scars. We are stuck on
opposite sides of the car, a couple of
molecules stuck in a rod of light
rapidly moving through darkness. He has
or my white eye imagines he has
the casual cold look of a mugger,
alert under hooded lids. He is wearing
red, like the inside of the body
exposed. I am wearing old fur, the
whole skin of an animal taken and
used. I look at his raw face,
he looks at my dark coat, and I don't
know if I am in his power —
he could take my coat so easily, my
briefcase, my life —
or if he is in my power, the way I am
living off his life, eating the steak
he may not be eating, as if I am taking
the food from his mouth. And he is black
and I am white, and without meaning or
trying to I must profit from his darkness,
the way he absorbs the murderous beams of the
nation's heart, as black cotton
absorbs the heat of the sun and holds it. There is
no way to know how easy this
white skin makes my life, this
life he could break so easily, the way I

imagine his own life is being broken, the
rod of his soul that at birth was dark and
fluid, rich as the heart of a seedling
ready to thrust up into any available light.

The Solution

Finally they got the Singles problem under control, they made it scientific. They opened huge Sex Centers – you could simply go and state what you want and they would find you someone who wanted that too. You would stand under a sign saying *I Like to be Touched and Held* and when someone came and stood under the sign saying *I Like to Touch and Hold* they would send the two of you off together.

At first it went great. A steady stream of people under the sign *I Like to Give Pain* paired up with the steady stream of people from under *I Like to Receive Pain. Foreplay Only – No Orgasm* found its adherents, and *Orgasm Only – No Foreplay* matched up its believers. A loyal Berkeley, California policeman stood under the sign *Married Adults, Lights Out, Face to Face, Under a Sheet*, because that's the only way it was legal in Berkeley – but he stood there a long time in his lonely blue law coat. And the man under *I Like to be Sung to While Bread is Kneaded on My Stomach* had been there weeks without a reply.

Things began to get strange. The *Love Only – No Sex* was doing fine; the *Sex Only – No Love* was doing really well, pair after pair walking out together like wooden animals off a child's ark, but the line for *38D or Bigger* was getting unruly, shouting insults at the line for *8 Inches or Longer*, and odd isolated signs were springing up everywhere, *Retired Schoolteacher and Parakeet – No Leather; One Rm/No Bath/View of Sausage Factory.*

The din rose in the vast room. The line under *I Want to be Fucked Senseless* was so long that portable toilets had to be added and a minister brought in for deaths, births and marriages on the line. Over under *I Want to Fuck Senseless –*

no one, a pile of guns. A hollow roaring filled the enormous gym. More and more people began to move over to *Want to be Fucked Senseless*. The line snaked around the gym, the stadium, the whole town, out into the fields. More and more people joined it, until *Fucked Senseless* stretched across the nation in a huge wide belt like the Milky Way, and since they had to name it they named it, they called it the American Way.

I Go Back to May 1937

I see them standing at the formal gates of their colleges,
I see my father strolling out
under the ocher sandstone arch, the
red tiles glinting like bent
plates of blood behind his head,
I see my mother with a few light books at her hip
standing at the pillar made of tiny bricks with the
wrought-iron gate still open behind her, its
sword-tips black in the May air,
they are about to graduate, they are about to get married,
they are kids, they are dumb, all they know is they are
innocent, they would never hurt anybody.
I want to go up to them and say Stop,
don't do it – she's the wrong woman,
he's the wrong man, you are going to do things
you cannot imagine you would ever do,
you are going to do bad things to children,
you are going to suffer in ways you have not heard of,
you are going to want to die. I want to go
up to them there in the late May sunlight and say it,
her hungry pretty blank face turning to me,
her pitiful beautiful untouched body,
his arrogant handsome face turning to me,
his pitiful beautiful untouched body,
but I don't do it. I want to live. I
take them up like the male and female
paper dolls and bang them together
at the hips like chips of flint as if to
strike sparks from them, I say
Do what you are going to do, and I will tell about it.

What If God

And what if God had been watching, when my mother
came into my room, at night, to lie down on me
and pray and cry? What did He do when her
long adult body rolled on me
like lava from the top of the mountain
and the magma popped from her ducts, and my bed
shook from the tremors, the cracking of my nature
across? What was He? Was He a bison
to lower His partly extinct head
and suck His Puritan phallus while we cried
and prayed to Him, or was He a squirrel
reaching through her hole in my shell, His arm
up to the elbow in the yolk of my soul
stirring, stirring the gold? Or was He
a kid in Biology, dissecting me
while she held my split carapace apart
so He could firk out the eggs, or was He a man
entering me while she pried my spirit
open in the starry dark —
she said that all we did was done in His sight
so He must have seen her weep, into my
hair, and slip my soul from between my
ribs like a tiny hotel soap, He
washed His hands of me as I washed my
hands of Him. Is there a God in the house?
Is there a God in the house? Then reach down
and take that woman off that child's body,
take that woman by the nape of her neck like a young cat
and lift her up, and deliver her over to me.

The Blue Dress

The first November after the divorce
there was a box from my father on my birthday – no card, but
big box from Hink's, the dark
department store with a balcony and
mahogany rail around the balcony, you could
stand and press your forehead against it
until you could almost feel the dense
grain of the wood, and stare down
into the rows and rows of camisoles,
petticoats, bras, as if looking down
into the lives of women. The box
was from there, he had braved that place for me
the way he had entered my mother once
to get me out. I opened the box – I had
never had a present from him –
and there was a blue shirtwaist dress
blue as the side of a blue teal
disguised to go in safety on the steel-blue water.
I put it on, a perfect fit,
I liked that it was not too sexy, just a
blue dress for a 14-year-old daughter the way
Clark Kent's suit was just a plain suit for a reporter, but I
felt the weave of that mercerized Indian Head cotton
against the skin of my upper arms and my
wide thin back and especially the skin of my
ribs under those new breasts I had
raised in the night like earthworks in commemoration of his
    name.
A year later, during a fight about
just how awful my father had been,
my mother said he had not picked out the dress,

just told her to get something not too expensive, and then
had not even sent a check for it,
that's the kind of man he was. So I
never wore it again in her sight
but when I went away to boarding school
I wore it all the time there,
loving the feel of it, just
casually mentioning sometimes it was a gift from my father,
wanting in those days to appear to have something
whether it was true or a lie, I didn't care, just to
have something.

After 37 Years My Mother Apologizes for My Childhood

When you tilted toward me, arms out
like someone trying to walk through a fire,
when you swayed toward me, crying out you were
sorry for what you had done to me, your
eyes filling with terrible liquid like
balls of mercury from a broken thermometer
skidding on the floor, when you quietly screamed
Where else could I turn? Who else did I have?, the
chopped crockery of your hands swinging toward me, the
water cracking from your eyes like moisture from
stones under heavy pressure, I could not
see what I would do with the rest of my life.
The sky seemed to be splintering like a window
someone is bursting into or out of, your
tiny face glittered as if with
shattered crystal, with true regret, the
regret of the body. I could not see what my
days would be, with you sorry, with
you wishing you had not done it, the
sky falling around me, its shards
glistening in my eyes, your old soft
body fallen against me in horror I
took you in my arms, I said *It's all right,
don't cry, it's all right*, the air filled with
flying glass, I hardly knew what I
said or who I would be now that I had forgiven you.

First Love

For Averell

It was Sunday morning, I had the *New York*
Times spread out on my dormitory floor, its
black print coming off dark silver on the
heels of my palms, it was spring and I had the
dormer window of my room open, to
let it in, I even had the radio
on, I was letting it all in, the
tiny silvery radio voices – I
even let myself feel that it was Easter, the
dark flower of his life opening
again, his life being given back
again, I was in love and I could take it, the ink
staining my hands, the news on the radio
coming in my ears, there had been a wreck
and they said your name, son of the well-known
they said your name. Then they said where they'd
taken the wounded and the dead, and I called the
hospital, I remember kneeling by the
phone on the third-floor landing of the dorm, the
dark steep stairs down
next to me, I spoke to a young
man a young doctor there in the
Emergency Room, my open ear
pressed to the dark receiver, my open
life pressed to the world, I said
Which one of them died, and he said your name,
he was standing there in the room with you
saying your name.
                    I remember I leaned my
forehead against the varnished bars of the
baluster rails and held on,

pulling at the rails as if I wanted to
pull them together, shut them like a dark
door, close myself like a door
as you had been shut, closed off, but I could not
do it, the pain kept coursing through me like
life, like the gift of life.

Greed and Aggression

Someone in Quaker meeting talks about greed and aggression
and I think of the way I lay the massive
weight of my body down on you
like a tiger lying down in gluttony and pleasure on the
elegant heavy body of the eland it eats,
the spiral horn pointing to the sky like heaven.
Ecstasy has been given to the tiger,
forced into its nature the way the
forcemeat is cranked down the throat of the held goose,
it cannot help it, hunger and the glory of
eating packed at the center of each
tiger cell, for the life of the tiger
and the making of new tigers, so there will
always be tigers on the earth, their stripes like
stripes of night and stripes of fire-light –
so if they had a God it would be striped,
burnt-gold and black, the way if
I had a God it would renew itself the
way you live and live while I take you as if
consuming you while you take me as if
consuming me, it would be a God of
love as complete satiety,
greed and fullness, aggression and fullness, the
way we once drank at the body of an animal
until we were so happy we could only
faint, our mouths running, into sleep.

It

Sometimes we fit together like the creamy
speckled three-section body of the fruit,
and sometimes it is like a blue comb of glass across my skin,
and sometimes I am bent over, as thick paper can be
folded, on the rug in the center of the room
far from the soft bed, my knuckles
pressed against the grit in the grain of the rug's braiding where
   they
laid the rags tight and sewed them together,
my ass in the air like a lily with a wound on it,
and I feel you going down into me as
if my own tongue is your cock sticking
out of my mouth like a stamen, the making and
breaking of the world at the same moment,
and sometimes it is sweet as children we had
thought were dead being brought to the shore in the
long boats, boatload after boatload.
Always I am stunned to remember it,
as if I have been to Saturn or the bottom of a trench in the sea
   floor, I
sit on my bed the next day with my mouth open and think of it

Topography

After we flew across the country we
got in bed, laid our bodies
delicately together, like maps laid
face to face, East to West, my
San Francisco against your New York, your
Fire Island against my Sonoma, my
New Orleans deep in your Texas, your Idaho
bright on my Great Lakes, my Kansas
burning against your Kansas your Kansas
burning against my Kansas, your Eastern
Standard Time pressing into my
Pacific Time, my Mountain Time
beating against your Central Time, your
sun rising swiftly from the right my
sun rising swiftly from the left your
moon rising slowly from the left my
moon rising slowly from the right until
all four bodies of the sky
burn above us, sealing us together,
all our cities twin cities,
all our states united, one
nation, indivisible, with liberty and justice for all.

I Cannot Forget the Woman in the Mirror

Backward and upside down in the twilight, that
woman on all fours, her head
dangling and suffused, her lean
haunches, the area of darkness, the flanks and
ass narrow and pale as a deer's and those
breasts hanging down toward the center of the earth
    like plummets, when I
swayed from side to side they swayed, it was
so dark I couldn't tell if they were gold or
plum or rose. I cannot get over her
moving toward him upside down in the mirror like a
fly on the ceiling, her head hanging down and her
tongue long and black as an anteater's
going towards his body, she was so clearly a human
animal, she was an Iroquois scout creeping
naked and noiseless, and when I looked at her
she looked at me so directly, her eyes so
dark, her stare said to me I
belong here, this is mine, I am living out my
true life on this earth.

Little Things

After she's gone to camp, in the early
evening I clear our girl's breakfast dishes
from the rosewood table, and find a small
crystallized pool of maple syrup, the
grains standing there, round, in the night, I
rub it with my fingertip
as if I could read it, this raised dot of
amber sugar, and this time
when I think of my father, I wonder why
I think of my father, of the beautiful blood-red
glass in his hand, or his black hair gleaming like a
broken-open coal. I think I learned
to love the little things about him
because of all the big things
I could not love, no one could, it would be wrong to.
So when I fix on this tiny image of resin
or sweep together with the heel of my hand a
pile of our son's sunburn peels like
insect wings, where I peeled his back the night before camp,
I am doing something I learned early to do, I am
paying attention to small beauties,
whatever I have – as if it were our duty to
find things to love, to bind ourselves to this world.

Looking at Them Asleep

When I come home late at night and go in to kiss the
    children,
I see our girl with her arm curled around her head,
her face deep in unconsciousness – so
deeply centered she is in her self,
her mouth slightly puffed like one sated but
slightly pouted like one who hasn't had enough,
her eyes so closed you would think they have rolled the
iris around to face the back of her head,
the eyeball marble-naked under that
thick satisfied desiring lid,
she lies on her back in abandon and sealed completion,
and the son in his room, oh the son he is sideways in his
    bed,
one knee up as if he is climbing
sharp stairs up into the night,
and under his thin quivering eyelids you
know his eyes are wide open and
staring and glazed, the blue in them so
anxious and crystally in all this darkness, and his
mouth is open, he is breathing hard from the climb
and panting a bit, his brow is crumpled
and pale, his long fingers curved,
his hand open, in the center of each hand
the dry dirty boyish palm
resting like a cookie. I look at him in his
quest, the thin muscles of his arms
passionate and tense, I look at her and see a
face like the face of a snake who has swallowed a deer,
content, content – and I know if I wake her she'll
smile and turn her face toward me though

half asleep and open her eyes and I
know if I wake him he'll jerk and say Don't and sit
up and stare about him in blue
unrecognition, oh my Lord how I
know these two. When love comes to me and says
What do you know, I say This girl, this boy.

The Glass

I think of it with wonder now,
the glass of mucus that stood on the table
in front of my father all weekend. The tumor
is growing fast in his throat these days,
and as it grows it sends out pus
like the sun sending out flares, those pouring
tongues. So my father has to gargle, cough,
spit a mouthful of thick stuff
into the glass every ten minutes or so,
scraping the rim up his lower lip
to get the last bit off his skin, then he
sets the glass down on the table and it
sits there, like a glass of beer foam,
shiny and faintly golden, he gargles and
coughs and reaches for it again
and gets the heavy sputum out,
full of bubbles and moving around like yeast —
he is like a god producing food from his own mouth.
He himself can eat nothing, anymore,
just a swallow of milk, sometimes,
cut with water, and even then
it can't always get past the tumor,
and the next time the saliva comes up
it is ropy, he has to roll it in his throat
a minute to form it and get it up and dis-
gorge the oval globule into the
glass of phlegm, which stood there all day and
filled slowly with compound globes and I would
empty it and it would fill again
and shimmer there on the table until
the room seemed to turn around it

in an orderly way, a model of the solar system
turning around the sun,
my father the old earth that used to
lie at the center of the universe, now
turning with the rest of us
around his death, bright glass of
spit on the table, these last mouthfuls.

The Lifting

Suddenly my father lifted up his nightie, I
turned my head away but he cried out
Shar!, my nickname, so I turned and looked.
He was sitting in the high cranked-up bed with the
gown up, around his neck,
to show me the weight he had lost. I looked
where his solid ruddy stomach had been
and I saw the skin fallen into loose
soft hairy rippled folds
lying in a pool of folds
down at the base of his abdomen,
the gaunt torso of a big man
who will die soon. Right away
I saw how much his hips are like mine,
the long, white angles, and then
how much his pelvis is shaped like my daughter's,
a chambered whelk-shell hollowed out,
I saw the folds of skin like something
poured, a thick batter, I saw
his rueful smile, the cast-up eyes as he
shows me his old body, he knows
I will be interested, he knows I will find him
appealing. If anyone had told me I would sit
by him and he'd pull up his nightie and I'd look
at him, at his naked body, at the thick
bud of his glans, his penis in all that
dark hair, look at him
in affection and uneasy wonder,
I would not have believed it. But now I can still
see the tiny snowflakes, white and
night-blue, on the cotton of the gown as it
rises the way we were promised at death it would rise,
the veils would fall from our eyes, we would know everything.

The Race

When I got to the airport I rushed up to the desk,
bought a ticket, ten minutes later
they told me the flight was canceled, the doctors
had said my father would not live through the night
and the flight was canceled. A young man
with a dark brown mustache told me
another airline had a non-stop
leaving in seven minutes. See that
elevator over there, well go
down to the first floor, make a right, you'll
see a yellow bus, get off at the
second Pan Am terminal, I
ran, I who have no sense of direction
raced exactly where he'd told me, a fish
slipping upstream deftly against
the flow of the river. I jumped off that bus with those
bags I had thrown everything into
in five minutes, and ran, the bags
wagged me from side to side as if
to prove I was under the claims of the material,
I ran up to a man with a white flower on his breast,
I who always go to the end of the line, I said
Help me. He looked at my ticket, he said
Make a left and then a right, go up the moving stairs and
    then
run. I lumbered up the moving stairs,
at the top I saw the corridor,
and then I took a deep breath, I said
Goodbye to my body, goodbye to comfort,
I used my legs and heart as if I would
gladly use them up for this,

to touch him again in this life. I ran, and the
bags banged me, wheeled and coursed
in skewed orbits, I have seen pictures of
women running, their belongings tied
in scarves grasped in their fists, I blessed my
long legs he gave me, my strong
heart I abandoned to its own purpose,
I ran to Gate 17 and they were
just lifting the thick glossy
lozenge of the door to fit it into
the socket of the plane. Like the one who is not
too rich, I turned sideways and
slipped through the needle's eye, and then
I walked down the aisle toward my father. The jet
was full, and people's hair was shining, they were
smiling, the interior of the plane was filled with a
mist of gold endorphin light,
I wept as people weep when they enter heaven,
in massive relief. We lifted up
gently from one tip of the continent
and did not stop until we set down lightly on the
other edge, I walked into his room
and watched his chest rise slowly
and sink again, all night
I watched him breathe.

The Feelings

When the intern listened to the stopped heart
I stared at him, as if he or I
were wild, were from some other world, I had
lost the language of gestures, I could not
know what it meant for a stranger to push
the gown up along the body of my father.
My face was wet, my father's face
was faintly moist with the sweat of his life,
the last moments of hard work.
I was leaning against the wall, in the corner, and
he lay on the bed, we were both doing something,
and everyone else in the room believed in the Christian God,
they called my father *the shell on the bed*, I was the
only one there who knew
he was entirely gone, the only one
there to say goodbye to his body
that was all he was, I held hard
to his foot, I thought of the Eskimo elder
holding the stern of the death canoe, I
let him out slowly into the physical world.
I felt the dryness of his lips under
my lips, I felt how even my light
kiss moved his head on the pillow
the way things move as if on their own in shallow water,
I felt his hair rush through my fingers
like a wolf's, the walls shifted, the floor, the
ceiling wheeled as if I was not
walking out of the room but the room was
backing away around me. I would have
liked to stay beside him, ride by his
shoulder while they drove him to the place where they would
     burn him,

see him safely into the fire,
touch his ashes in their warmth, and bring my
finger to my tongue. The next morning,
I felt my husband's body on me
crushing me sweetly like a weight laid heavy on some
soft thing, some fruit, holding me
hard to this world. Yes the tears came
out like juice and sugar from the fruit —
the skin thins and breaks and rips, there are
laws on this earth and we live by them.

Beyond Harm

A week after my father died
suddenly I understood
his fondness for me was safe – nothing
could touch it. In that last year,
his face would sometimes brighten when I would
enter the room, and his wife said that
once, when he was half asleep,
he smiled when she said my name. He respected
my spunk – when they tied me to the chair, that time,
they were tying up someone he respected, and when
he did not speak, for weeks, I was one of the
beings to whom he was not speaking,
someone with a place in his life. The last
week he even said it, once,
by mistake. I walked into his room and said,
'How are you,' and he said, 'I love you
too.' From then on, I had
that word to lose. Right up to the last
moment, I could make some mistake, offend him,
and with one of his old mouths of disgust he could
re-skew my life. I did not think of it much,
I was helping to take care of him,
wiping his face and watching him.
But then, a while after he died,
I suddenly thought, with amazement, he will always
love me now, and I laughed – he was dead, dead!

Waste Sonata

I think at some point I looked at my father
and thought *He's full of shit*. How did I
know fathers talked to their children,
kissed them? I knew. I saw him and judged him.
Whatever he poured into my mother
she hated, her face rippled like a thin
wing, sometimes, when she happened to be near him,
and the liquor he knocked into his body
felled him, slew the living tree,
loops of its grain started to cube,
petrify, coprofy, he was a
shit, but I felt he hated being a shit,
he had never imagined it could happen, this drunken
sleep was a spell laid on him –
by my mother! Well, I left to them
the passion of who did what to whom, it was a
baby in their bed they were rolling over on,
but I could not live with hating him.
I did not see that I had to. I stood
in that living room and saw him drowse
like the prince, in slobbrous beauty, I began
to think he was a kind of chalice,
a grail, his love the goal of a quest,
yes! He was the god of love
and I was a shit. I looked down at my forearm –
whatever was inside there
was not good, it was white stink,
bad manna. I looked in the mirror
and as I looked at my face the blemishes
arose, like pigs up out of the ground
to the witch's call. It was strange to me

that my body smelled sweet, it was proof I was
demonic, but at least I breathed out,
from the sour dazed scum within,
my father's truth. Well it's fun talking about this,
I love the terms of foulness. I have learned
to get pleasure from speaking of pain.
But to die, like this. To grow old and die
a child, lying to herself.
My father was not a shit. He was a man
failing at life. He had little shits
traveling through him while he lay there unconscious –
sometimes I don't let myself say
I loved him, anymore, but I feel
I almost love those shits that move through him,
shapely, those waste fetuses,
my mother, my sister, my brother, and me
in that purgatory.

Acknowledgements

The poems in this selection are taken from the following books, to whose publishers acknowledgement is made: *Memo for Spring* (Reprographia, 1972), *The Grimm Sisters* (Next Editions, 1981), *Dreaming Frankenstein and Collected Poems* (Polygon, 1984), *Bagpipe Muzak* (Penguin, 1991) and *Three Scottish Poets: MacCaig, Morgan, Lochhead* (Cannongate, 1992) for Liz Lochhead; *Melting into the Foreground* (Viking, 1986) and *Defying Gravity* (Viking, 1992) for Roger McGough; *Satan Says* (The University of Pittsburgh Press, 1980), *The Dead and the Living* (Knopf, 1984), *The Gold Cell* (Knopf, 1987) and *The Father* (Knopf, 1992) for Sharon Olds.